French Words

MODERN LANGUAGES IN PRACTICE

Series Editor:
Michael Grenfell, *Centre for Language in Education, University of Southampton.*

Editorial Board:
Do Coyle, *School of Education, University of Nottingham.*
Simon Green, *Trinity & All Saints College, Leeds.*

Editorial Consultant:
Christopher Brumfit, *Centre for Language in Education, University of Southampton.*

The Modern Languages in Practice Series provides publications on the theory and practice of modern foreign language teaching. The theoretical and practical discussions in the publications arise from, and are related to, research into the subject. *Practical* is defined as having pedagogic value. *Theoretical* is defined as illuminating and/or generating issues pertinent to the practical. Theory and practice are, however, understood as a continuum. The series includes books at three distinct points along this continuum: (1) Limited discussions of language learning issues. These publications provide an outlet for coverage of actual classroom activities and exercises. (2) Aspects of both theory and practice combined in broadly equal amounts. This is *the core of the series*, and books may appear in the form of collections bringing together writers from different fields. (3) More theoretical books examining key research ideas directly relevant to the teaching of modern languages.

Other Books in the Series
Cric Crac! Teaching and Learning French through Story-telling
    Roy Dunning
Effective Language Learning
    Suzanne Graham
Foreign Language and Culture Learning from a Dialogic Perspective
    Carol Morgan and Albane Cain
Fluency and its Teaching
    Marie-Noelle Guillot
The Elements of Foreign Language Teaching
    Walter Grauberg
The Good Language Learner
    N. Naiman, M. Fröhlich, H.H. Stern and A. Todesco
Inspiring Innovations in Language Teaching
    Judith Hamilton
Le ou La? The Gender of French Nouns
    Marie Surridge
Motivating Language Learners
    Gary N. Chambers
New Perspectives on Teaching and Learning Modern Languages
    Simon Green (ed.)
Switched On? Video Resources in Modern Language Settings
    Steven Fawkes
Target Language, Collaborative Learning and Autonomy
    Ernesto Macaro
Training Teachers in Practice
    Michael Grenfell
Validation in Language Testing
    A. Cumming and R. Berwick (eds)

Please contact us for the latest book information:
Multilingual Matters, Frankfurt Lodge, Clevedon Hall,
Victoria Road, Clevedon, BS21 7HH, England
http://www.multilingual-matters.com

MODERN LANGUAGES IN PRACTICE 14
Series Editor: Michael Grenfell

French Words
Past, Present and Future

Malcolm Offord

MULTILINGUAL MATTERS LTD
Clevedon • Buffalo • Toronto • Sydney

To Judith, whom words cannot describe

Library of Congress Cataloging in Publication Data

A catalog record for this book is available from the Library of Congress.

British Library Cataloguing in Publication Data

A catalogue entry for this book is available from the British Library.

ISBN 1-85359-497-0 (hbk)
ISBN 1-85359-496-2 (pbk)

Multilingual Matters Ltd

UK: Frankfurt Lodge, Clevedon Hall, Victoria Road, Clevedon BS21 7HH.
USA: UTP, 2250 Military Road, Tonawanda, NY 14150, USA.
Canada: UTP, 5201 Dufferin Street, North York, Ontario M3H 5T8, Canada.
Australia: P.O. Box 586, Artarmon, NSW, Australia.

Typeset by Archetype-IT Ltd (http://www.archetype-it.com).
Printed and bound in Great Britain by Cambrian Printers Ltd.

Contents

Introduction

French words have exerted an irresistible fascination on French speakers for many centuries – not only on those for whom it is a native language but also on those who learn and speak it as a foreign language, for pleasure or for more serious purposes. Hundreds of dictionaries of the French language have been compiled, and many studies have been devoted to the way the words of French have evolved and come to assume the forms and meanings they have today. Over the centuries the language has acquired a mystique, which has led certain experts to want to preserve it in as pure a form as possible, to discourage innovation and to ensure that all users conform to a standard usage. The intention of these experts is to keep the language free from what they consider to be the contamination of foreign influences and the ill-formed creations invented by contemporary users. However, no living language can avoid change, especially one which is the vehicle of a vibrant, multi-facetted culture. Indeed French is undergoing constant change – new words are coming into existence on a daily basis, and that from a variety of sources. These new words are added to the stock of words which are enshrined in the dictionaries, so that the French vocabulary is a wonderful mixture of old and new, of lexical comings and goings; in many ways a reflection of the history of the French people.

The purpose of this book is to uncover the ways in which French words 'work', by approaching them from as many angles as possible. The first two chapters are devoted to discussing what a word is and examining how meaning is conveyed. Chapter 1 *Words and Their Constituent Parts* shows that the word is not necessarily the smallest unit of meaning. In this chapter those elements which combine together to form French words are identified and an attempt is made to classify them and discover what properties they have in common and which ones distinguish them. The second chapter *Words* examines more closely what the word 'word' actually means. A distinction is drawn between orthographic words and vocabulary items, before consideration is given to the relationships which words enter into with each other. These involve mainly sense relationships, in which words are seen as units making up a variety of integrated semantic networks, some of which are narrow in scope, others of which proliferate into many ramifications. A number of patterns of meaning are also focused on – synonymy, antonymy, hyponymy (all explained in the appropriate places!). Another relationship explored in this chapter is that based on the form of words – two words with the same form create ambiguity, known as homonymy: the origins, types and effects are analysed.

The next two chapters pose the question, 'Where do French words come from?' Chapter 3, *Words With a Long History*, as its title suggests, tries to answer the question by concentrating upon those words which entered the language many centuries ago, mainly from Latin, and which in many ways form the bedrock of the present-day language. By examining a number of laws which affected the way Latin words were pronounced in Gaul, an attempt is made to explain the shape of contemporary words and their relationships with their lexical ancestors. Chapter 4, *Words With a Foreign Origin,* approaches the question about where French words come from from a different angle, looking at those languages which have donated words to French. The means whereby such words reach French are examined before the contributor languages are reviewed. The chapter concludes with a chart showing which languages have made the greatest contributions to French.

The final chapter, Chapter 5, *Words With a Short History,* asks where French words are going. It looks at the ways in which the French vocabulary is being extended at the present time. The processes of morphological renewal – principally derivation, composition, shortening – are discussed and illustrated, as well as the ways in which old words at times acquire new meanings.

Instead of using pages of conventional discursive text to narrate the story of French words, the material is divided up into what are hoped are easily assimilated 'text-bites'. The material in each chapter is presented in a series of frames. These are organised according to a type of hierarchy. Frames with thick lines contain definitions, frames with verticals the main thrust of the material and the examples, whilst frames with dotted borders contain questions. Answers to the questions are sometimes provided in the Appendix; sometimes they occur in the text itself or are easy to deduce from the text; sometimes there is no particular answer, and the question is there to prompt debate. It is hoped that you will find the presentation of the material attractive and easy to access. The use of headings for the text-bites tells you immediately what the substance of that box actually is. They also help signpost the drift of the individual chapters – so, if you wish to skip a particular section, you are free to do so (and almost invited to do so in Chapter 3!). You will be able to see exactly what it is you are missing – as well as have a convenient way of recalling what you have read.

Chapter 1

Words and Their Constituent Parts

For many centuries it was accepted that the **word** was the smallest unit of meaning in a language. However, when linguists began to examine closely the nature and composition of words, they were obliged to revise this notion and replaced it by one which states that the **smallest significant unit in a language is the morpheme**.

Morpheme

A **morpheme** is the minimal distinctive unit of grammar, i.e. morphemes carry information which is morphological and / or semantic.

NB. morphological = relating to word structure; semantic = relating to meaning.

Morphemes combine together to form words, although, as we shall see, some words consist of only one morpheme.

Example 1: A noun
- *Empoisonneurs* results from the addition of a prefix (*em*) to a stem (*poison*) with adjustment of the spelling to fit pronunciation (*n*), followed by a suffix marking agent (*eur*) and an ending (*s*) marking plural number; the semantic information comes principally from the stem and the prefix, the morphological information comes from the ending and also the suffix.

Example 2: A verb
- *Repousserons* involves the addition of a prefix (*re*) to a stem (*pouss*) with a suffix (*er*) which marks the infinitive and provides the basis for the future tense and an inflectional ending (*ons*) indicating third person plural.

However, consideration of many French words will quickly prove that identification of morphemes sometimes presents problems. **The structure of certain words is transparent, that of others is opaque, that of yet others hovers between transparency and opacity.** It is obviously much more straightforward to analyse into their constituent parts words that are transparent than those that are opaque, where the divisions between the parts is virtually indiscernible.

Examples of transparent words
- If you know the meaning of *ouvre* from *ouvrir* and the meaning of *boîte*, then

1

there is a good chance that you can deduce the meaning of the compound word *ouvre-boîte*.

- Again, if you know the meaning of *transport* and if you know that the suffix *-eur* is used to form derivatives meaning that someone or something is carrying out the action described by the stem, then you can work out the meaning of *transporteur*.

- With a degree of imagination added to your linguistic knowledge, a word like *baladeur* = 'walkman' also becomes transparent.

Transparency

A word is said to be transparent if its component parts are easily identifiable and if their combined meanings allow speakers to arrive at a successful decision as to the meaning of the original word.

Opacity

A word is said to be opaque if it is impossible to piece together its meaning from its constituent parts; indeed it may not always be obvious that a word is made up of constituent parts.

These opaque situations usually arise for historical reasons relating to the ways in which sounds change over the centuries, but also because elements drop out of use or change their original meanings (see Chapter 3).

Examples of opaque words
- Although *oeil* and *yeux* look as if they are made up of completely different elements, and you probably instinctively thought that there was a link between them, it is not until you trace their histories back to their Latin origins that you can affirm with certainty that they actually derived from different forms of the same Latin word – *oculum* and *oculos*, from *oculus*. The transparent link between the Latin forms has been lost in the passage into French.

- The Latin word *pedem* = 'foot' was the basis for a large number of Latin words, the connections between which were transparent to Latin speakers. However, in the course of time, as those words developed into French, their relatedness became more and more opaque. Who would guess, without a knowledge of their Latin roots, that *pied, piètre, pédestre, piège, empêcher, piéton, pion* are ultimately connected?

Transparency and opacity are two extremes of a gradient. Many words exhibit degrees of one or the other, and discerning the components of many words is a subjective, individual matter, depending amongst other things upon our knowledge of Latin, our intuitions, our logic.

> *Example of degrees of transparency / opacity*
> - You would probably agree that the link between *pied* and *piéton* is much closer than that between *pied* and *empêcher* (the original meaning of which was 'to restrain someone by holding onto their foot').

French words are very prone to opaque word-structure, and this complicates the type of analysis which we are about to embark upon. However, opacity is not the only problem which arises from the fact that French is an old language which has been in a constant state of evolution since early medieval times. Another major related problem, concerning particularly the spoken language, is the fact that the pronunciation of modern French is very different from what it was a thousand years ago, when French first appeared as an independent language. This would not be so serious if the spelling of modern French had kept pace with changes in pronunciation. Unfortunately that has not happened, and the spelling system in use today reflects not so much the way that the French of the twenty-first century is pronounced as the way French was pronounced many centuries ago. The result is that there is often a wide discrepancy between the spelling and the pronunciation of modern French, especially as far as word endings are concerned.

> *Examples of the spelling / pronunciation discrepancy*
> - The expression of number in adjectives, nouns and pronouns:
>   Is it possible to distinguish between the pronunciations of the following pairs? – *jeune / jeunes, grande / grandes, homme / hommes, femme / femme, il / ils, elle / elles.* The answer is – no.
>
> - Verb endings -
>   With verbs the situation is even more acute. Four persons of the present indicative tense of *-er* verbs and two of *-ir* verbs sound exactly the same, although they are spelt differently – *chante / chantes / chante / chantent; finis / finit.*
>   This also applies in varying degrees to the imperfect and conditional tenses of all verbs.

The Classification of Morphemes

There are many different types of morphemes. In the light of what has just been said, it should be clear that a morphemic analysis of French is an extremely delicate operation, and that the language does not lend itself to neat classification from this point of view. This of course makes the exercise that much more challenging! It should also be admitted that in what follows some explanations of processes have been simplified and historical explanations of current situations ignored. The aim of this chapter is to indicate the main features associated with French word-structure and to enable you to dissect words into their constituent parts, their morphemes. At times it will be instructive to engage in both **an orthographic and an oral presentation**.

The first distinction that needs to be drawn is between **free** and **bound** morphemes.

Free morphemes

> Free morphemes can occur on their own as complete words in their own right and will normally feature as separate entries in a dictionary.

Bound morphemes

> Bound morphemes need to be combined with other morphemes and cannot occur as individual items; nor do they possess morphological or semantic independence. They are not normally recorded as separate entries in a dictionary.

Examples of free morphemes
- *Petit, cousin, quand, pour* are free morphemes, independent words, recorded in dictionaries; they cannot be reduced to form smaller items. No words consisting entirely of parts of these words exist. The first two can be added to: for example *petit* can have *e* added to it to form the feminine and / or *s* to form the plural; similarly *cousin* can become feminine by the addition of *e* and plural by the addition of *s*; they can also be used to create compound words, such as *petit-cousin, petit-beurre,* but they cannot be subtracted from.

Bound morphemes constitute a much more heterogeneous group of items.

Examples of bound morphemes
- The *-e* and *-s* mentioned above are bound morphemes, changing the morphological role of the two nouns; verb endings perform a similar function for verbs; the *-esse* in *petitesse,* changing the word-class of the adjective to that of a noun, is another bound form.

1. Free morphemes

Free morphemes are **independent words** which can stand as words in their own right. This category involves only those words which consist of a single morpheme (monomorphemic words) which cannot be further split into other free morphemes. Most word-classes are involved.

Examples of word classes and free morphemes
- Most prepositions and conjunctions: *après, devant, en, et, mais, sur* (*à* and *de* will receive special comment later).
- Most adjectives in the masculine singular form and also those feminine ones which have the same form as the masculine: *chic, fort, laid, vrai* (but see below for those ending in *e*).
- Many nouns in the singular form: *arc, chien, océan, soupçon.*
- A few adverbs: *bien, tard, tôt, très*; but no verbs.

Words ending in *e* need special consideration and are a good illustration of the difference between a morphemic analysis based upon spelling and one based upon pronunciation. The final *e*, present in spelling for historical reasons, is often deleted in order to form certain derivatives, with the consequence that, from an orthographic point of view, these words fit into the following category (bound morphemes) rather than this one.

> ### Example of the treatment of -e
> - *sage* becomes reduced to *sag-*, which then becomes the base upon which derivatives such as *sagesse* and *assagir* are constructed.
> - However, this distinction is not relevant in an oral analysis, since /saʒ/ represents the root with or without *e*.

2. Bound morphemes

Bound morphemes can be divided into a number of sub-categories.

2.1. Non-independent stems

These are normally the bases upon which other words are constructed by adding other bound morphemes to them. The difference between this group of morphemes and the preceding one is that this group cannot stand alone but requires the addition of another morpheme to form fully-fledged words. It should be stressed that there are many anomalies and irregularities when it comes to deconstructing French words into stems. These may generally be accounted for by reference to the morphological history of the French language and will therefore not detain us here. Suffice it to say that this sometimes means that certain words have more than one stem (but see Chapter 3). These variant stems are sometimes discernible only in the written form and not in the oral form and sometimes show only minimal variation. Another result of this situation is that, in the orthographic form, the same morpheme may sometimes function as an independent word, as in 1 above, and sometimes, after slight adjustment, as a non-independent stem, as here: in other words it may be both an independent word and a non-independent stem.

> ### Example of word and stem fluctuation in the written form
> - In the case of *roi* / *royal*, *roi* is an independent word which becomes the non-independent stem *roy-* when used as the base for *royal* (and *royaume*, *royauté*).

Occasionally even more radical stem alternation occurs: this will be examined later.

Non-independent stems arise among the following word classes.

> ### Examples of word classes and bound morphemes: 1
> - **All verbs:** in the case of regular verbs (of the types *porter*, *finir* / *partir*, *vendre*), the stem is invariable and provides the base upon which all the other forms of the verb are constructed, e.g. for *porter*: *je port-e*, *je port-ais*, *je port-er-ai*, *j'avais port-é*.

- However, in the case of irregular verbs, the stem is variable, indeed highly variable for some verbs (this is clear in the oral form, but the phonetic distinction may sometimes be scarcely audible), e.g. *lever: lev- / lèv-, jeter: jet- / jett-, pouvoir: peu- / pouv- / peuv- / pou- / pu- / pui-, savoir: sai- / sav- / sau- / sach-, aller: v- / all- / i- / aill-; être: s- / e- / ét- / f- / soy-.*

Examples of word classes and bound morphemes: 2

- **Some adjectives and nouns:** it is with adjectives and nouns that the distinction between a phonetic and orthographic approach becomes critical. In some cases the orthographic and phonetic versions of the stem are identical, e.g. *angl + ais, compl + et, glac + ial, heur + eux / euse, révél + ateur.*
- However, in others, exclusively when a final *e* is concerned, the outcome of the two analyses is quite different, as the next table shows.
- Other adjectives present particular problems, e.g. *beau / bel / belle, fou / fol / folle* (in these two cases the stem simply consists of a single sound, *b-* and *f-*).
- In other cases, a noun derived from an adjective produces different stems, e.g. *tiède > tièd-* and *tiédeur > tiéd-.* At times understanding the link requires, if not a deep knowledge of historical circumstances (see Chapter 3 for guidance), at least a fertile imagination, e.g. *chauve / calvitie, frêle / fragilité.*

Examples of different results of phonetic and orthographic analyses

- The treatment of final *e* –
  orthographic analysis
  larg + e (élargir), maussad + e (maussaderie), montsr + e
  phonetic analysis
  / larʒ / , / mosad / , / mɔ̃str/
- Other adjectives present particular problems with stem variation –
  blanc / blanche, frais / fraîche, sec / sèche, vieux / vieil / vieille.

Sometimes the link between the noun and its derivative is far removed, and in some cases the link becomes almost unrecognisable, e.g. *femme / féminin, église / ecclésiastique, loi / légal.*

2.2. Derivational morphemes

Prefixes, suffixes and infixes, which do not have an independent existence, may be added to the front, end and middle respectively of other words or morphemes to create new words. Prefixes and suffixes are discussed in more detail in Chapter 5.

Examples of infixation

- *-r- / -rr-* to form the future and conditional tenses of all verbs.
- *if- / -ifi-, -is-* to form verbs from certain nouns, e.g. *liquide > liquidifier, standard > standardiser.*

Examples of prefixation

- By adding prefixes to *mettre* a number of new verbs may be formed, e.g. *ad- + mettre > (produces) admettre; dé- + mettre > démettre.*

Exercise 1

Can you think of any other words derived from *mettre* by the addition of a prefix?

Examples of suffixation

- By adding suffixes (and infixes) to *fort* a number of new words may be formed – *fort + e + ment, fort + ifi + -er*.

Exercise 2

Can you think of any other words derived from *fort* by the addition of a suffix?

Exercise 3

What new words can you create from *froid, long* using prefixes and suffixes?

Exercise 4

Divide up the following words according to the roots, prefixes and suffixes involved.

capitalisme, déshumaniser, ensoleillé, retombée, rigoureusement, surabondance.

2.3. Inflectional morphemes

Morphemes indicating **gender** and **number** may be added to adjectives and nouns, others indicating **person, number** and **tense** may be added to verbs. As with derivational morphemes, it sometimes happens that an adjustment has to be made to the stem or original word. This is especially the case with verbs.

Gender

Exercise 5

What morphemes indicate feminine gender for adjectives? Give examples involving stem variation too.

Exercise 6

What morphemes indicate feminine gender for nouns?

Of course, there are a few cases where the feminine form appears to be a shortened form of the masculine (or the masculine is derived from the feminine!).

> *Examples*
> • *compagnon / compagne, dindon / dinde, garçon / garce.*

Number

> *Exercise 7*
>
> What morphemes indicate plural number for nouns and adjectives? Remember to distinguish between phonetic and orthographic representations.

But remember that certain nouns and adjectives are invariable in the plural

> *Examples*
> • Nouns ending in *s, x, z* – *mois, souris, choix, nez,* and certain adjectives borrowed from other languages – *open* (in sport), *sexy, snob.*

Remember also that the plural of *oeil* is *yeux.*

> *Exercise 8*
>
> What morphemes indicate plural number for verbs? Again remember to distinguish between phonetic and orthographic representations.

Person

> *Exercise 9*
>
> Taking *donner* and *finir* as your examples, show what morphemes indicate the persons of verbs. Yet again remember to distinguish between phonetic and orthographic representations.

Tense

> *Exercise 10*
>
> Taking *porter* and *salir* as your examples, show how morphemes indicate the various tenses of French verbs. For the last time, remember to distinguish between phonetic and orthographic representations.

Exercise 11

It was said above that stem variation (orthographic and / or phonetic) is common amongst verbs to indicate different tenses, e.g. *croire: croi-, croy-*.

Using the previous example as a model, show what stem variation is involved in the following verbs – *asseoir, avoir, conduire, faire, lécher, vouloir*.

Can you think of any others which manifest stem variation?

3.4. Special cases

Definite articles: *le, la, les*. The most logical way to analyse the definite articles is to treat *l-* (not *le*) as the stem, with + *e* or + *a* for masculine and feminine singular and + *es* for the plural of both genders (not *-s* for masculine and *-es* for feminine).

Partitive articles (and *de* + definite articles): *du, de la, des*. It is best to consider *de* and *d-* as examples of stem variation; consequently *du* = two morphemes, *de la* = three morphemes, *des* = two morphemes.

Exercise 12

Analyse *à* in combination with the definite articles.

Chapter 2

Words

Identifying and defining a word has always presented problems not only to the everyday speaker but also to the linguist, and there is no universally agreed definition available. Problems arise because of the multifarious nature of words and the inconsistent ways in which speakers use the word *word*. Let us consider some of the issues involved and attempt to arrive at a satisfactory working definition for our purposes, starting with a definition that applies only to words in their written form.

A definition

Words are separated from each other by spaces when they occur in a piece of text (writing).

Validity test applied to a short text
  – Vos parents, comment vivaient-ils?
  – C'est formidable. Ils ont vécu un amour fou, une passion. Mes parents m'ont appris en même temps la liberté. Ma mère avait deux hommes, mon père et moi, simplement. Mes parents ont vécu avec un grand respect l'un pour l'autre.

- If we count those words occurring between spaces, we discover that there are 44 items. These are known as **graphological units**.

However, instinctively we feel that the passage contains more words than that, and it is clear that other factors need to be taken into account.

Complicating factors 1 – The apostrophe effect
- In French a finite number of very short words ending in -*e* (known as mute e) elide the -*e* before a word beginning with a vowel, the place of the elided -*e* being indicated by an apostrophe. The list of such words comprises –
    le, me, te, se, que, ne, de, ce.
- In addition *la* acts in the same way.
- *Si* elides its vowel before *il* / *ils* only.
- If the elided words in the passage are noted and treated as normal words, the number of items increases by four, to 48.

Complicating factors 2 – The hyphen effect 1

- This is triggered by the presence of a hyphen in *vivaient-ils*. It is the practice in French that when an interrogative is formed by inversion of the subject and the verb, the subject pronoun is linked to the verb by a hyphen, as in this case. Consequently, another item is to be added to the list, making 49.

The hyphen effect 2

- However, the use of a hyphen in French does not always signal that a subject pronoun has been appended to a verb. Hyphens are used in other circumstances as well, when in fact separate items are not indicated.
- This applies, for example, when *même* is attached to a personal pronoun (for example *moi-même*) and also in the formation of many compound expressions (for example *gratte-ciel, ouvre-boîte, (une fusée) sol-air*), all of which would count as single words (but see below).
- A hyphen also occurs in constructions when the letter *t* is used to indicate that in speech a *t* sound has been inserted between a verb-ending involving a vowel and a pronoun beginning with a vowel (for example *a-t-il fait cela?*). In word counts it is normal to ignore the *-t-*.

The total we have reached is the number of word forms or **orthographic words** in the passage.

It is possible to look at the passage in another way, and to count the number of different words in the passage, the **vocabulary items**.

Vocabulary items

- *parents, ont* and *un* occur three times each in the passage, and *mes, l'* and *vécu* twice each. That means that, although there are 49 distinct orthographic words in the passage, there are 40 different vocabulary items.

Combining the orthographic words and vocabulary items

- By grouping together the different orthographic forms of the same vocabulary item, the word-counting process can be taken a stage further.
- For example, *vivaient* and *vécu* are both manifestations of the base vocabulary item, the infinitive *vivre*. Indeed it makes sense to include the whole of the form of the perfect tense of *vivre*, in other words including the auxiliary, *ont vécu*, under that heading.
- A similar situation applies to the feminine and masculine forms of the indefinite article, *un* and *une*, which are subsumed under the masculine singular form *un*, and also to the possessive adjectives *mon, ma* and *mes* which are likewise subsumed under the masculine singular form *mon*.
- This allows us to delete another nine forms from the vocabulary items list, which now makes 31 different words.

Base forms

- In French it is traditional to treat masculine forms as the standard, base form, when it comes to dealing with the singular / plural forms of nouns or the singular / plural or masculine / feminine forms of adjectives and so on, and to use infinitives as the base form when it comes to regrouping the different parts of verbs.

Subsuming and close family likeness

- Subsuming words under the appropriate vocabulary item is usually straightforward. There is generally a 'family likeness' between the various word forms involved. In the passage we have *un / une*.
- Other examples are *donne / donnons / donnent / donnai / donnerai*, etc. or *cheval / chevaux, vache / vaches, grand / grande*.

Exercises

How many other forms belong under the vocabulary item *donner?*

List the forms belonging under the items *connaître, recevoir, vouloir*.

What special problems arise from listing the forms associated with *aller, avoir, être, pouvoir?*

Suppletion and verb forms

- In the case of *vécu* and *vivre*, already mentioned, the two words have only a *v* in common.
- More extreme examples are provided by certain highly irregular verbs, as you may have discovered in the exercises: *avoir* with future and conditional tenses in *aur-*, with a past participle in *eu* and many other forms beginning with that combination of letters; *être* with …– and you have already noted them – in fact only *êtes*, past participle *été*, imperfect tense beginning *ét.* „.bear any resemblance to the infinitive; the other forms – *suis, es, est, sommes, sont, sois*, etc., *serai*, etc., *fus* etc. – are highly disguised forms of the verb! The same applies to *aller*.

Exercises

Can you think of yet other verbs to which this applies?

Can you think of any other parts of speech to which it also applies? (Hint – think of how *good, better, best* of English would be translated into French.)

Suppletion and other word classes

- The previous examples have involved verbs. Other word classes are also involved, where the link between the various forms is based solely upon meaning.

(1) In some cases the words have the same ultimate Latin or Greek origin but have diverged with the passage of time, producing forms which no longer appear linked in modern French. Nouns and the corresponding adjectives are often involved here.

Examples

lieu / local, loi / légal, mère / maternel, mois / mensuel.

(2) In yet other cases, the two words derive from different original forms and suppletion reaches breaking point.

Examples

jour / quotidien, lettre / épistolaire, sud / méridional, ville / urbain.

Exercises

Can you think of any other examples of type 1? What about the French for words to do with 'father, night, nose, peace, ripe, spirit'?

The recording of suppleted forms in dictionaries

- The question arises as to whether such forms merit separate entries in a dictionary or whether they should be included under the base form. The practice of standard dictionaries is varied: they tend not to record individual forms of verbs when suppletion occurs. Consequently looking for *serai* is a frustrating exercise – it will not be found as such; its location is under the headword *être*. However, *meilleur, mieux, pire, pis* are entered separately.

Exercises

Can you think why verbs and adverbs should be treated differently?

Is the status of the latter different from that of verbs?

How are articles and pronouns treated in dictionaries?

The practice in word-counting

- It is normal in a word-count to treat all forms of a verb, however diverse they may be, as one vocabulary item; articles and pronouns should be treated similarly.
- On the other hand, comparative and superlative forms of adjectives, linked adjectives and nouns may be treated as individual items.

Exercise

Make a word-count of the following passage: provide a figure for the number of orthographic words and the number of vocabulary items. Pay special attention to the apostrophes and hyphens. How would you deal with proper names?

Vendredi matin vers 5 heures, à Toulouse, Geneviève Gonzalez, 32 ans, sortait d'une boîte de nuit quand elle a vu la voiture d'Alexis Favarel, 20 ans, plonger dans le canal de Brienne. La jeune femme n'a pas hésité à se jeter à l'eau pour le délivrer du véhicule. Les sapeurs-pompiers ont transporté le jeune homme, très choqué, à l'hôpital Purpan.

Treatment of du

- What we have here is an orthographic word which consists of two vocabulary items, *de* and *le* (see Chapter 1). Therefore, in a word-count, it is necessary to treat the orthographic form as a single occurrence, but, in the calculation of the vocabulary items, to break it down into its constituent elements.

The first passage also throws up another issue, which might affect the word count, namely the difference between **content words** and **function words**.

Content words

Content words are the nouns, adjectives, verbs and adverbs which carry most of the meaning of a sentence, whereas **function words** are the other word-classes, prepositions, conjunctions, articles, pronouns and so on, which perform principally a syntactic function.

The former are the bricks of a building, giving it its structure and architecture, the latter the mortar holding the bricks together, essential but less noticeable.

The ambivalence of certain forms

- The distinction between content words and form words is generally easy to apply, but there is one instance in the passage where the distinction might be missed. It involves the two values of *avoir*, shown in *ils ont vécu un amour fou* and *ma mère avait deux hommes*.
- In the first case *ont* is an example of the use of *avoir* as a function word, specifically its use as an auxiliary verb creating the past tense of most French verbs.
- In the second case *avoir* is being used as a content verb with its full meaning of 'to have'. In terms of the word count, *avoir* as a content word is counted as a vocabulary item, whereas *avoir* as a function word is subsumed under the verb *vivre* and is not counted.

Having examined some of the idiosyncrasies associated with words – the distinction between orthographic words and vocabulary items, the use of the apostrophe and hyphen, the existence of suppletion, the distinction between form and content words – we return to our original question: is it possible to define a word? The answer is 'yes' – provided that the definition is very flexible and provided that we are allowed to make certain exceptions!

A word is a minimum free form (definition, part 1)

A word is a minimum free form (expression first formulated by the American linguist Leonard Bloomfield in 1926 and generally adopted subsequently). What is meant by **minimum**?

This means that the word is the smallest unit of meaning that can be used on its own; it cannot be divided into smaller units which can stand independently by themselves.

Example
- *goût* is a word by this definition, because it cannot be divided into smaller units.
- *goûter* is also a word by this definition, because, although it can be broken down into the morphemes *goût + er*, the latter has no independent existence.
- Similarly *dégoût* and *dégoûter* are words, because again the prefix *dé* has no independent existence.

Exception
- However, there is a group of words which fall foul of this aspect of the definition, namely compound words, e.g. *casse-croûte* = snack, *protège-cahier* = protective cover for exercise-book, because each of the constituent parts is another free form.

A word is a minimum free form (definition, part 2)

A word is a minimum free form. What is meant by **free**?

This means that the word enjoys certain properties, namely that it has **positional mobility and internal stability and has an identifiable semantic or syntactic function**.

Positional mobility means that the word is not permanently attached to a word like a derivational prefix but can occur in various positions in a sentence, etc. **Internal stability** means that it has a permanent form, although this will have to accommodate a certain amount of inflectional and derivational variation.

The definition applies best to content words, less well to function words, as their internal stability is often minimal (e.g. the definite articles, forms of possessive adjectives and so on).

Lexical Item / Lexeme

Having recognised some of the difficulties inherent in the definition of a word, it is desirable to refine our terminology. We have seen above that it is important to distinguish between an **orthographic word** and a **vocabulary item**. More convenient than the term 'vocabulary item' is **lexical item** or **lexeme** to describe the smallest distinctive unit in the semantic system (vocabulary or lexicon (see below)) of a language.

It is important to realise that **words are rarely used in isolation**. They form relationships with other words in various ways, as the following sections illustrate.

Lexeme (definition 1)

A **lexeme** may consist of a single word, e.g. *crème, machine*. But it may also consist of two words, e.g. *crème brûlée, crème dépilatoire* = hair-removing cream, *crème fouettée* = whipped cream, *machine-outil* = machine tool, *machine totalisatrice* = totaliser, *machine composée* = compound machine; three words, e.g. *crème au beurre* = butter cream, *machine à coudre* = sewing machine, *machine à écrire* = typewriter, and so on, e.g. *machine à traitement de texte* = word processor. What is important is not so much the number of words involved as the fact that together they form a single semantic entity.

Lexeme (definition 2)

The term **lexeme** is also used to denote the base form of words which undergo suppletion (e.g. *le, mon* are considered to be lexical items, whereas *la, ma, les, mes* are word forms). These base forms have an abstract quality and are the forms which generally appear as headwords in dictionaries.

Exercises

Find some lexemes consisting of two, three, four and five orthographic words.

Collocation

Collocation

Some words are more likely to occur in the same context than others. In other words, **words habitually co-occur**. There is a high degree of predictability that the same words will be found in similar contexts. As soon as one of a group of such words occurs, we can expect with a high degree of certainty that one or some of the others will also occur in that context.

Examples

- It is more likely, for example, that *charbon* = coal, *exploiter* = to mine, *gisement* = stratum, *mine*, *sécurité* = safety will be found in the same context than, for example, *charbon, chien , vélo, église, politique*.
- If we use the word *professeur*, it is very likely that words such as *élève, enseigner* will occur in the vicinity, rather than *plaisir, chocolat, évêque*.

Exercises

Find 10 more lexical items that are likely to collocate with *professeur*.

Find 10 more lexical items that are unlikely to collocate with *professeur*.

Cluster

Cluster

Lexical items that collocate form clusters. Clusters are groups of lexical items that habitually co-occur.

Examples

- *professeur, élève, enseigner* and the other 10 items you found form a **cluster**, whereas *plaisir, chocolat, évêque* and the other 10 items you found probably do not.

Exercise 1

Find 6 items which form the cluster 'those who teach and those who are taught'.

Find 10 items which form the cluster 'teaching establishments'.

Find 10 items which form the cluster 'the teaching / learning process'.

Find 10 items which form the cluster 'equipment for teaching'.

Exercise 2

Starting with the lexical item *voiture* gather as many other items that you can think of relating to a car.

Form them into clusters.

Lexical Sets and Semantic Fields

Clusters which are closely linked to each other form lexical sets.

Sometimes it is convenient to posit other, higher levels, as necessary, in the lexical hierarchy. (Compare the following example on sport.)

Lexical items that collocate form clusters; closely linked clusters form lexical sets; **lexical sets themselves are subdivisions of semantic fields**.

The label **semantic fields** is a very general one which enables us to classify and organise the whole of a language's **lexicon** (see below).

Examples
- Clusters such as teaching personnel, teaching establishments, teaching equipment, the teaching / learning processes form the lexical set education.
- The lexical sets mammals, rodents, birds, amongst others, form part of the semantic field animals.

Exercise

What name should we give to the lexical set and semantic field formed by vehicles, parts of a car, roads, the driving process, etc?

Lexis

Lexis

The vocabulary of a language is known by linguists as its **lexis**; the lexical items forming clusters forming lexical sets build up to form the lexis of a language.

Lexicon

Lexicon

The complete inventory of a language's **lexis** is known as its **lexicon**. This corresponds in the printed form to a **dictionary** containing all the language's lexical items.

Example
- What follows is a worked example of part of a semantic field subdivided into lexical sets, then into clusters and then into lexical items within clusters. The analysis is by no means exhaustive. At the end, see if you can add more detail to the tables.

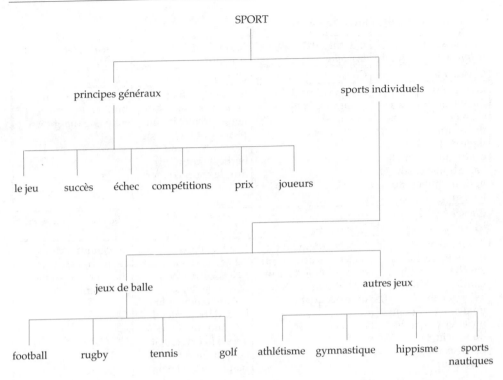

Principes généraux

Cluster 1 le jeu	Cluster 2 le succès	Cluster 3 l'échec	Cluster 4 les compétitions	Cluster 5 les prix	Cluster 6 les joueurs
faire du sport, jouer, faire de l'exercice, les exercices, être sportif, pratiquer un sport, s'entraîner	surpasser, vaincre, le succès, réussir, gagner, une victoire, un triomphe, le vainqueur, décrocher le titre, le gagnant, battre, reléguer à la seconde place, le champion, une réussite, être premier	échouer, ne pas réussir, un échec, perdre, être perdant, rater, tomber à plat, être dernier	une compétition, un tournoi, un concours, un match, une partie	une récompense, récompenser, un prix, accorder un prix, décerner un prix, un prix en espèces, une médaille de bronze, d'argent, d'or, une trophée, gagner des points	un sportif, une sportive, un concurrent, une équipe, un arbitre, un athlète, un footballeur, un rugbyman, un tennisman, un nageur

Sports individuels – jeux de balle

Lexical set 1 le football	Lexical set 2 le rugby	Lexical set 3 le tennis	Lexical set 4 le golf
Cluster 1 le terrain	*Cluster 1 le terrain*	*Cluster 1 le court*	*Cluster 1 le terrain*
le corner, les poteaux de but, la zone des six mètres, la surface de réparation, la ligne de touche, le centre du terrain, la barre transversale, la ligne du milieu du terrain	la ligne d'essai, les montants, la ligne médiane	un court, le filet, la ligne de service, la ligne de côté, le simple, le double, le double mixte, le court sur herbe, le court en dur, le court couvert	le tee, le trou, un bunker, le fairway, le green, le rough
Cluster 2 les positions	*Cluster 2 les positions*	*Cluster 2 le jeu*	*Cluster 2 l'équipement*
l'avant-centre, le demi-centre, l'inter gauche / droit, le gardien de but, un ailier gauche / droit, un demi, un buteur, un joueur du milieu du terrain, la défense, un défenseur	le pack, un demi de mêlée, les avants, un demi d'ouverture = fly half, un arrière, un trois-quart	le set, la partie, servir, le service, la volée, zéro, trente zéro, égalité, le volant, envoyer la balle dans le filet, le let, jouer un let, le revers = backhand, le coup droit = forehand drive, la balle de set / de match	les cannes / clubs – as in English, le caddie, une poussette pour cannes de golf
Cluster 3 le jeu	*Cluster 3 le jeu*	*Cluster 3 l'équipement*	
le coup d'envoi, marquer, commettre une faute, un coup interdit = foul, tacler, le but, marquer un but, le penalty, une faute, le centre = pass, mettre la balle en touche, un coup franc, tirer, shooter, arrêter le ballon, la prolongation = extra time, le match nul, plaquer	la pénalité, taper en touche, marquer un essai, une mêlée, former une mêlée, une rentrée en touche	la raquette, la balle, le filet, un bandeau / poignet = sweatband	

Sports individuels – les autres jeux

Lexical set 1 *athlétisme*	Lexical set 2 *gymnastique*	Lexical set 3 *hippisme*	Lexical set 4 *sports nautiques*
Cluster 1 *les épreuves*	*Cluster 1* *les épreuves*	*Cluster 1* *les épreuves*	*Cluster 1* *les épreuves*
une course, le cent mètres, le cent mètre haies, le saut en hauteur / en longueur, le triple saut, le saut à la perche, le javelot, le disque, le lancement du poids / du marteau, le marathon, le 1500 mètres, le relais, l'éliminatiore = heat	les cours de gymnastique, l'haltérophilie = weightlifting, les poids et haltères = weight training, l'aérobic, l'exercice	les sports équestres, le saut d'obstacles, le dressage, le gym-khana, la chasse au renard, le polo, une course de chevaux, les courses	le water polo, le surf, la planche à voile, la polongée sous-marine, la plongée avec un tuba, le canoë, l'aviron, la natation, la longueur, la brasse, le crawl, la brasse papillon, le dos crawlé, un plongeon
Cluster 2 *la performance*		*Cluster 2* *la performance*	*Cluster 2* *la performance*
courir, sauter, lancer, le sprint, éliminer, écraser, établir un record, battre le record du monde, un tour de piste		monter à cheval, aller au pas, trotter, au trot, aller au petit galop, galoper, franchir un obstacle	surfer, nager, plonger, flotter

Exercise 1

Examine the following lexical items, some of which you will already have produced yourself in a previous exercise, and distribute them among the clusters which are also given.

établissements scolaires – matières – équipement – personnel – processus éducatif – examens et tests – qualifications

agrégation, allemand, anglais, apprendre, archéologie, biologie, botanie, cahier d'exercices, certificat, chargé de cours, chimie, classe de première, classe, classes préparatoires, collège, collégien, conférence, copie d'examen, cour de récréation, cours, craie, devoirs, directeur, directrice, dirlo, doctorat, école, école maternelle, école d'Etat, école polytechnique, école primaire, école privée, école technique, écolier, éducation, éducation physique, éduquer, élève, enseignant, enseignement, enseignement supérieur, enseigner, épreuve, érudit, espagnol, établissement d'enseignement secondaire, étude, étudiant, étudiant de troisième cycle, étudier, examen, examinateur, faire un cours, faire des études, faire passer un examen à quelqu'un, former, français, garderie, géographie, histoire, institut, instituteur, instructeur, instruction, instruction religieuse, instruire, intellectuel, internat, interrogation, interroger, jardin d'enfants, laboratoire, laboratoire de langues, langues vivantes, leçon, lettres classiques, licence ès lettres, licence ès sciences, linguistique, lycée, lycéen, manuel, mathématiques, matière, matières littéraires, maître, moniteur, musique, obtenir sa licence / son diplôme / son bac, passer un examen, premier cycle, professeur d'université , philosophie, physique, pupitre, principal, professeur, qualification, rater, recteur, ne pas être reçu, réussir, réviser, salle de classe, savant, sciences, sciences économiques, sciences humaines, scolaire, en sixième, sociologie, sujet, surveillant, tableau noir, en terminale, test, test d'aptitude, travailler, universitaire, université.

Exercise 2
    Examine the semantic field TRANSPORT and create your own lexical sets with their clusters and lexical items.

Other Associations Between Words

In addition to structuring a language's lexis according to semantic themes, based on clusters, lexical sets and semantic fields, it is also possible to identify other patterns into which the lexis enters. These patterns are based upon a variety of types of associations or relations

Synonymy

> **Synonymy**
>
> Synonymy involves words with identical or almost identical meanings, words which are interchangeable in all or almost all circumstances.

Absolute synonymy
- It is extremely rare to meet synonyms which are absolutely identical and which can replace each other in each and every situation.

Exercise
    Why do you think absolute synonymy is so unusual?

- *Absolute synonymy goes counter to two of the great principles of linguistics –*
    (1) that languages are constructed on differences – we are so used to the idea that words have different meanings that if we are presented with two words that are supposedly synonymous, we try to discover a difference between them;
    (2) that languages are efficient and economical instruments – unnecessary words would clutter our mental lexicons. Having words with exactly the same meaning would serve no useful purpose (except perhaps to allow orators and writers to embellish their language more effectively). The vocabulary of French is so large in any case that words that are not really necessary, because their meaning may be conveyed by others, would be a luxury that our minds could ill afford to store. Speakers need to be able to draw fine distinctions between objects, qualities, states, and **partial synonyms** facilitate that need, whereas absolute synonyms would not.

Examples of absolute synonymy in modern French
- Despite the above, there are cases of **absolute synonymy** in every-day French, but not many, e.g. *deuxième / second, bicyclette / vélo*.

- Ironically, a number of absolute synonyms survive in scientific terminology. For example, in the realm of phonetics, mute *e* may be referred to as *e muet, sourd, caduc, féminin* in French.
- But it is in the area of **slang** that the greatest concentrations of absolute synonyms are to be found.
- To name the head, the following terms are a selection of those available from just two letters of the alphabet – *balle, bille, boule, caboche, citrouille, coco.*

Exercise
   Why should slang be so amenable to the production of absolute synonyms?

Partial synonymy
- Often the reason why absolute synonymy does not exist is that words have meanings which carry many nuances and expressive differences which are not exactly matched by another word, or there is some syntactic constraint which allows the synonyms to be distinguished.
- Consequently the majority of synonyms are **partial synonyms**.

Example 1
- The lexical items *avoir peur / craindre* are as close as can be to being absolute synonyms, but it is their **syntactic differences** which prevent that being achieved: *avoir peur* cannot replace *craindre* in *il n'y rien à craindre.*

Example 2
- What usually distinguishes synonyms is their **different expressive values**. *vieux monsieur* is more polite than *vieil homme; vieillard* suggests respect, *mon vieux* affection, whereas low register expressions like *barbe grise* are pejorative.

Exercise 1
   Here are a number of words associated with praise, with their values given in random order. Try to link the word with its appropriate value: *compliment, éloge, encens, louange, panégyrique* – praise + esteem, praise + judgement (positive or negative), praise + exaggeration, praise + flattery, moderate praise.

Exercise 2
   Try to distinguish in the same way as in *Exercise 1* between the following partial synonyms, remembering that some may be neutral and others have a more restricted application – *clair, limpide, net, propre, pur.*

Exercise 3

Briser and *casser* are partial synonyms. A series of contexts follows. With which expressions can both verbs be used, with which only one? –

une assiette, un bras, le coeur de quelqu'un, la croûte, une fenêtre, une glace, une grève, un traité, l'unité, un verre, une vitre.

Try to draw a general conclusion.

The effect of ageing

- Quite often one of a pair of absolute synonyms becomes less common in current usage and may eventually disappear altogether. Such words acquire an archaic ring – *choir = tomber, ouïr = entendre, quérir = chercher.*

Exercise

What are the current equivalents of *ardoir, maints*?

There are a number of ways in which synonyms may be distinguished.

Distinction between synonyms 1

- According to time of origin –

  In French, pairs of partial synonyms have resulted from the fact that they have been borrowed from the same language at different times.

Examples

frêle, froid, nourriture, raide, sûreté entered the language in the normal way from Vulgar Latin words (see Chapter 3); however, from the 14th century onwards the same Latin words were resorted to to produce the following synonyms, *fragile, frigide, nutrition, rigide, sécurité.*

Distinction between synonyms 2

- According to place of origin –

  As far as foreign influences are concerned, in the Renaissance period (16th century) the Italian words *cantatrice* and *cavalcade* were introduced into the language, thus creating synonyms for the earlier words *chanteuse* and *chevauchée.*

  More recently English has contributed to the formation of pairs of synonyms through the borrowing of such words as *interview* alongside the previous *entrevue, lunch* alongside *goûter, ticket* alongside *étiquette.*

  It also happens that in different parts of the country different words are used as alternatives to the standard French term.

Examples

Around Saint-Etienne *amiteux* = affectionate; near the border with Belgium *ducasse, kermesse* are used to denote local fairs (*fête*); in the South (but also more generally) *fada* = mad; in the Haute-Marne *département herbages* = weeds; in the west of the country *magette* = bean; in the South *mas* = farm; in the Lyon area *tantôt* = afternoon.

- On a broader scale, in different parts of the French-speaking world, words which are not current in the French of France are used as alternatives to standard terms.

Examples

In Canada *faire une application* = to apply, *chéquer* = to check, *chum* = mate, *espérer* = to wait, *fin de semaine* = weekend, *magasinage* = shopping, *traversier* = car ferry; in parts of Africa *charbon* = charcoal, *charlatan* = soothsayer, faith healer, *compéter* = to compete, *dévierger* = to rape, *petit français* = gibberish, *goudron* = tarmacked road, *graine* = peanut (Senegal), *gros mot* = elegant expression.

Distinction between synonyms 3

- According to register – slang
  Slang provides a very rich variety of words synonymous with standard French ones.

Examples

Almost every part of the body has at least one slang alternative term.

Exercises

What slang words do you know for parts of the body? (Don't be too squeamish!)

What is the theme running through the slang terms in the following list? –

bouche / gueule, bras / pattes, jambes / pattes, mourir / crever, nez / museau.

Slang also provides synonyms for many other aspects of daily life.

What are the standard French forms for the following slang words? –

bouffer, bouquin, fourrer, piocher, pieu.

Distinction between synonyms 4

- According to register – literary language
  At the other end of the register scale, literary or high-flown language often has recourse to high register terms rather than standard ones.

Examples

astre for *étoile*, *conférer* for *donner*, *coursier* for *cheval*, *firmament* for *ciel*, *impécunieux* for *pauvre*, *trépas* for *mort*.

Distinction between synonyms 5

- In specialised usage –
  There are also words used in particular specialist languages which are not

used in standard French. Professions, trades and other group activities create their own technical, specialist vocabularies.

Example

The medical profession uses *embolie* for *coup de sang*, *épiderme* for *peau*, *lésion* for *blessure*, *phlébotomie* for *saignée*, *phtisie* for *tuberculose*.

The use of the following synonyms is determined by the relevant political or legal context – *convention* is general in application, but *accord* implies the end of hostilities between rival groups; *contrat* is written and has a legal connotation; *pacte* is surrounded with a certain solemnity; *traité* is written and follows negotiations.

Distinction between synonyms 6

• According to connotation –

Sometimes one synonym has a neutral value, while the other or others have an affective quality.

Examples

enfant is neutral in value, as against *bambin*, *gosse*, *petit*, which tend to be positive, and *marmot*, *mioche*, *morveux*, which tend to be negative – but the speaker's tone can cancel out negative undertones!

In the synonymic pair *aimer* / *adorer*, the latter suggests passion and worship, whereas the former is more general.

In the pair, *cohue* / *foule*, the former suggests disorder and unruliness, while the latter again has no particular connotation.

Exercise

Can you detect any differences of connotation between the following pairs of synonyms? –

blesser / *estropier*, *regarder* / *toiser*, *nouveau* / *inédit*, *se maquiller* / *se peinturlurer*, *rusé* / *finaud*.

Distinction between synonyms 7

• The role of euphemism –

At times it is preferable not to refer directly to certain objects (parts of the body), events (death, illness), activities (drunkenness, sex) or bodily functions. Euphemisms come to the aid of the speaker who wishes to be circumspect in delicate circumstances and who needs to refer obliquely to a particular matter.

The buttocks = *fesses* are referred to euphemistically as *derrière* / *séant* / *arrière-train*; to die = *mourir* as *éteindre* / *avaler son bulletin de naissance* / *casser sa pipe* / *passer l'arme à gauche*.

• The colourful contribution made by slang to euphemisms is obviously extensive.

Synonymic values
- Synonyms may form a scale of values.

Example
> The amount of dislike experienced increases according to which of the following verbs is selected: *en vouloir, haïr, détester, exécrer.*

Exercises

Order the following words in terms of their intensity –

> *bête / dément / fou / idiot / naïf / stupide;*
> *crainte / effroi / épouvante / frayeur / peur / terreur;*
> *abattement / affliction / désespoir / désolation / mélancolie / tristesse.*

Can you detect any nuances of meaning between the following series of synonyms? –

> *cultivé, docte, érudit, intelligent, lettré, savant;*
> *affaibli, chétif, débile, faible, fragile, frêle, infirme;*
> *accomplir, achever, consommer, finir, parachever, terminer.*

Because certain – many – words have more than one meaning, they will have more than one set of synonyms, and synonyms of one meaning are not usually synonyms of the other(s).

Examples
- *sauvage* has *farouche* as a synonym with the meaning = wild (animal), but *inhabité* when it means = uninhabited (land);
- *bête* on the one hand (as a noun) has a synonym in *animal*, but on the other (as an adjective) *stupide*.
- *Farouche* and *inhabité, animal* and *stupide* may be synonyms of *sauvage* and *bête* respectively, but they are not synonyms of each other.

Antonyms

In addition to entering into synonymous relationships, words also enter into antonymous ones.

Antonymy

> Just as words may be associated with others through having similar meanings, they may also be associated with others through having **opposite or contradictory meanings.**

Examples
- The simplest way to form an antonym is to add a prefix with a negative value to the base word, e.g. *possible / impossible, conformiste / non-conformiste, accord / désaccord.*
- But more often a word unrelated in form and with an opposite meaning exists, e.g. *toujours / jamais, jeunesse / vieillesse, devant / derrière, noir / blanc, entrer / sortir.*

Antonyms 1 – Complementary antonyms
- Some antonyms are absolute and mutually exclusive, such as *mort / vivant, homme / femme,* so that the denial of one of the terms implies the assertion of the other. These are known as **complementary antonyms**.

Exercise
    Can you think of some other examples of complementary antonyms?

Antonyms 2 – Gradable antonyms
- Other antonyms are best viewed as stretching along a **scale from two opposing poles**, e.g. *beau / laid, riche / pauvre, jeune / vieux, grand / petit,* the point being that there are degrees of richness and poverty, etc. – just because you are not rich, you are not necessarily poor, you may be in-between!
- Similarly *jeune* in *jeune enfant* does not have the same value as it does in *jeune député* or *jeune octogénaire; grand* when applied to an insect has a different value from when it is applied to a mountain.
- Of course, sometimes an element of subjectivity colours the use that a certain speaker makes of a particular term, e.g. what (or whom) one person considers beautiful may be quite otherwise in another person's eyes.

Exercise
    The examples above all involved adjectives. Can you think of any adverbs, nouns or verbs which are similarly gradable?

Antonyms 3 – Converse / relational antonyms
- A third type of antonymy involves a relationship of **converseness or a relational opposition**. The two words involved are the converse of each other, e.g. *acheter* is the converse of *vendre* and vice versa, *recevoir* the converse of *donner, épouse* of *époux, oncle / tante* of *neveu / nièce.*

Homonymy

Whereas synonymy is based upon identity or quasi-identity of meaning between words, **homonymy** is based upon identity of form.

Examples
- There are many examples of **homonymy** in French, e.g. *balle* = ball / *balle* = bale, *louer* = to praise / *louer* = to hire.

Homonymy

The term **homonym** is usually reserved for groups of words whose spelling and pronunciation are identical but whose meanings are different.

However, there are many other groups of words with identical pronunciation but different spellings: these are called **homophones**.

Examples
    ceint (ceins) / cinq / sain / saint / sein / seing; vair / ver / verre / vers / vert.

There are a few other groups of words whose spelling is the same, but whose pronunciations vary; these are called **homographs**.

Examples
    est (cardinal point) / *(il) est, (nous) portions / (les) portions, reporter* (verb) / *reporter* (noun), *(le) sens / (je) sens.*

The shorter a word the more likely it is to have a homonym.

Homographs will be ignored in the ensuing discussion, and **homonyms** and **homophones** will be treated together, using the term homonym to denote both.

There are some significant points to note about homonyms.

Differentiating homonyms 1
- Homonyms may belong to different word classes.
Examples
    sans (preposition) / *sang* (noun), *vers* (preposition) / *vair, ver, verre, vers* (nouns) / *vert* (adjective).

Differentiating homonyms 2
- Homonyms may also be distinguished by gender.

Examples
>   *le / la livre, le / la page, le / la vase.*

Exercises

How many homonyms can you find with the following phonetic sequences? –

/fwa / , / ku / , / kur /, / mɛr / , / pɛr / ?

Find the masculine homonym corresponding to the following feminine ones –

la garde = protection, guards, *la manche* = sleeve, *la mousse* = moss, *la vague* = wave.

Find homonyms from different word classes for the following words –

bois = drink (verb), *boucher* = to plug, *dans* = in, *souris* = mouse, *tendre* = tender (adjective).

In the examples of homonyms, the lexical gap between the meanings of the two or more words involved has been considerable, and the danger of ambiguity resulting from such words sounding the same has been minimal, especially if there is a syntactic distinction between them (different genders or word-classes).

It should be pointed out that there is another linguistic phenomenon related to homonymy which involves the fact that many words have more than one meaning. This is known as **polysemy.**

Polysemy

> The situation where contained within a word's meaning are a number of nuances, usually closely related to each other but with slight differences. Some words have only a few nuances of this type, others many. The vaguer the word the more likely it is to have a large number of nuances.

Examples
- *écran* = screen may be applied to a vast range of very different screens, often with different functions, but having in common the fact that they are nonetheless screens, e.g. *écran de cinéma, de télévision, d'ordinateur, de fumée, solaire, crème écran total, anti-bruit.*
- Similarly, *appuyer* has a number of values which emerge depending upon its collocation or context – (1) to rest or lean against, e.g. *appuyer une échelle contre un mur,* (2) to lean on, e.g. *appuyer sur le bouton,* (3) to support (a candidate, team etc.), (4) to base (something upon something), e.g. *appuyer son raisonnement sur des faits nouveaux,* (5) to insist, e.g. *appuyer sur son opinion.*

Hyponymy

A last type of association is that of **hyponymy.**

Hyponymy

The inclusion of the meaning of one or more terms in that of another.

The latter is known as the **superordinate** term and the former as **co-hyponyms.**

Examples
- The names of specific flowers, **co-hyponyms,** such as *rose, tulipe, violette, orchidée* are all included in the more general name *fleur,* the **superordinate term**.
- The **superordinate** term *rouge* includes within its meaning such other colour terms as *carmin, cramoisi, écarlate, pourpre, vermeil,* **co-hyponyms.**

The word's wide web

It is clear from the foregoing that a word is at the centre of a large number of associations – like a spider, it sits amid a giant web of linked words, some clearly associated, some more tenuously.

The Number of Words in French

Having attempted to define what a word is and having examined all the ramifications involved in so doing, the logical next step is to speculate on the number of words there are in the French language. This time the controversy does not so much concern what is meant by a French word – although we have already seen the problems involved in defining a *word*, and there is also debate as to what is a *French* word (see Chapter 4) – as what is meant by the *French lexis* itself. It is more or less universally accepted that dictionaries are the guardians of the words of a language – dictionaries vie with each other in their claims to present the most complete inventory of a language's lexicon. French is particularly well served in this respect.

Trésor de la langue française
- The *Trésor de la langue française* (the first of sixteen volumes appeared in 1971), complemented by the *Trésor général des langues et parlers français* (neither of which has yet been completed), is probably the most ambitious lexicographical venture ever undertaken: the corpus gathered for these projects comprises about 260 million words, from which about 1,200,000 different French words have been recorded.

Larousse and Le Robert
- In addition French enjoys the privilege of two prestigious publishing houses which produce each year new editions of their families of dictionaries. The best known of these dictionaries and the most widely consulted are without doubt *Le Petit Robert*, which contains about 60,000 entries and *Le Petit Larousse* dictionary, which has about 76,000 entries.
- It scarcely needs to be pointed out that both of these contain only a small proportion of the words which the *Trésors* will eventually publish.

The extent of the average speaker's vocabulary
- Research has shown that the average French person draws on, for normal conversation, a stock of about 3,500 words: this is known as **le français élémentaire**.
- Indeed, it has been calculated that probably only 1,500 words are necessary for everyday communication, just over 1% of the *Trésors'* tally: this constitutes **le français fondamental** (established in 1958).
- There is, therefore, a phenomenal difference between the number of words which the average French speaker uses on a regular basis and the potential number of words in the lexicon.

The *Trésors* will contain every word that has ever been used in French in the documents they have analysed. The humbler dictionaries contain those words which are in fairly regular use – and, as Chapter 5 shows, new words are being created every day and adding to French's lexical stock. Consequently, all that can be said is that when you are discussing the size of the French lexis, the answer has to be carefully qualified – and the answer given one day will no doubt be different from that given the next!

Chapter 3

Words With a Long History

Despite the pretensions of purists, French is, like English, a mongrel of a language, with ingredients taken from many different sources. In fact, as we shall see, French has welcomed words from all continents into its vocabulary. This is a process which has been going on for many centuries, indeed ever since the emergence of French as an independent language. The following two chapters will attempt to supply information and examples about the way in which the language has developed and how it has acquired words from these varied sources – this chapter will concentrate upon the prehistory of the language and its formative period – and the next upon its subsequent development and foreign acquisitions.

The Situation Before the Arrival of the Romans

The Neolithic period
- Neolithic man, and maybe woman, left indications of their presence and artistic talents on the walls of caves and on megalithic monuments in a number of regions of France.
- Other inhabitants may well have come and gone without leaving any trace of their settlements and certainly without having any impact upon the subsequent development of the French language.

Ligurians, Iberians and Greeks
- The first peoples to leave any linguistic evidence, and that very slight, were the **Ligurians** and **Iberians**, who settled in the southern half of present-day France, and the **Greeks**, who settled along the Mediterranean coast.
- This evidence is mainly in the form of elements of place-names (in the case of Ligurian, for example *Venasque*, and in that of Greek, *Marseille, Nice, Antibes*) and also in words mediated by other dialects / languages and, in the case of Iberian, in the present-day Basque language.
- From Ligurian via various dialects came *alpage* = pasture, *marron* = chestnut, *chalet*.
- From Iberian via Spanish came *baraque* = hut, *givre* = frost, *joue* = cheek.
- Greek influence is preserved mainly in present-day Occitan rather than French, but *caler* = to wedge, *dôme, fantôme* and *trèfle* = clover originate from this period.

Exercises

Why do you think the linguistic offerings from Ligurian and Iberian are so few?

How would you explain why certain of these words are preserved in place-names and others have entered French through the intermediary of other dialects / languages?

The Gauls

The Gauls – early contact

- The **Ligurians** and **Iberians** were eventually displaced by the **Gauls**, who had begun their migrations west from eastern and central Europe in the 8th century BC and arrived in the country that was to bear their name around 500 BC.

The Gauls – early conflict

- The **Gauls** eventually came into conflict with **Greek settlers**, who had colonised the southern fringe of the country from 600 BC onwards. The reaction of the Greeks was to summon help from **Rome**, the most powerful state of the time.

Gaul and Rome – early campaigns

- (1) **Rome** was only too pleased to have an excuse to move across the Alps and establish a foothold for itself in Gaul. The first campaign into Gaul conducted by the Romans took place between 154 and 125 BC and concentrated upon the area settled by the Greeks. The result was the establishment of the Roman province known as *Provincia Narbonensis*, from which the present-day name *Provence* and the noun / adjective *provençal* derive.
- (2) The first campaign was followed nearly a hundred years later by a much larger enterprise, led by **Julius Caesar**, between 57 and 52 BC, which saw the whole of the rest of the country fall under Roman control and signalled the death-knell of Gaulish. Military invasion and action were followed by colonisation.

Exercise

Imagine the invasion of Gaul by the Romans. What sort of people would be involved – in the military campaigns and then as settlements were established?

Romanisation

The establishment and adoption of Roman practices by their conquered peoples. This was mainly an urban phenomenon, the countryside being comparatively unaffected early on and only slowly coming under Roman influence.

Exercises

Why would the previous inhabitants of Gaul be prepared to follow Roman ways?

Which Gauls would be most likely to do this?

Which ones might be more resistant to Roman influence?

The Gauls and romanisation
- It was in fact in the best interests of the Gauls to become romanised. All power and opportunities for intellectual, social, cultural and financial advancement lay in the hands of the Romans.
- Consequently ambitious Gauls were eager to acquire the language of their conquerors in order to provide for themselves a place in the sun.
- In some towns, schools and universities were established, where the sons of Gaulish aristocratic families could acquire a knowledge of Latin.

The Gaulish language
- **Gaulish** belongs to the Celtic group of languages and was spoken in Gaul for a period of about seven hundred years.
- By the 3rd century AD it was well on the way to being abandoned in favour of Latin.

The Gauls, Gaulish and Latin
- It should be emphasised that none of the schools mentioned above were available for ordinary people to be taught Latin. They had to pick the language up as best they could, with no one to correct them and no reliable models to follow. The Latin speakers they would come into contact with most often would be traders, soldiers, settlers from different parts of the Empire, all speaking with different accents, none of whom would make any effort to guide the Gauls in their language-learning endeavours.
- A long period of **bilingualism** preceded the disappearance of Gaulish from daily use by the end of the 5th century. From then onwards, Latin, influenced by Gaulish speech habits, was adopted throughout the country. The linguistic result of **the merging of Latin and Gaulish is known as Gallo-Roman**.

Gaulish linguistic influence upon French
- However, **Gaulish** did not disappear completely – there are still a few words of Gaulish origin surviving in modern French.
- These words, estimated to be 180 in all, relate to the **daily activities** of the Gauls. Some of the words are restricted to use in French, others passed into Latin and thence into other European languages.

Examples (a small selection)
- (1) Words which passed via Latin into other European languages – *cheval, chemise, changer, chemin.*
- (2) Words which occur only in French. This is a larger collection and comprises words relating mainly to: **agriculture** – *boue* = mud, *talus* = slope, *glaner* = to glean, *ruche* = beehive; **domestic matters** – *suie* = soot, *briser* = to break, *habiller;* **names of animals** – *bouc* = billy goat, *mouton* = sheep; **names of trees** – *bouleau* = birch, *if* = yew, *sapin* = fir.

Exercises

Comment on the word classes (e.g. nouns, verbs) involved.

Which ones are represented, which ones are absent? Can you suggest why?

Germanic

The Germans – early contact
- Germanic tribes began infiltrating Gaul from the end of the 2nd century AD and invading on a large scale from the 4th.
- The Alemans occupied the east (present-day Alsace), the Burgundians the area from the Franche-Comté to Savoy, the Visigoths the south.

The Franks
- Especially important were the **Franks**, who first occupied the north and then spread to the rest of the country north of the Loire.
- The Franks, who, as the Gauls had done before them, eventually bequeathed their name to the country, did not succeed in imposing their language upon the conquered population like the Romans.

Exercise

Can you suggest why the Franks' language was not adopted?

Reasons for the retention of Gallo-Roman
- (1) The occupation by the Franks was not sufficiently dense to ensure that the whole population came into contact with German speakers, and their culture was inferior to that already existing in the country.
- (2) The conversion of the Frankish king, Clovis, to Christianity in 426. Since Latin was the language of the Church, the conversion of the Franks meant that they became familiar with that language, an essential ingredient of Gallo-Roman.

The Frankish linguistic influence upon French
- The **Frankish** contribution to the vocabulary of emerging **Old French** was extensive, much more so than Gaulish, but many of the words are no longer in current use.
- It has been calculated that, whereas Old French contained about a thousand words of Germanic origin, only between three and four hundred survive into Modern French, of which about 150 are used regularly.

Exercise
Can you think why there should be such a loss of words?

Frankish linguistic influence upon French – semantic areas (a small selection)
- The major semantic areas covered by the Frankish contribution are:
  animals – *épervier* = sparrow-hawk, *guêpe* = wasp, *blaireau* = badger, *renard* = fox.
  plants – *blé* = corn, *framboise* = strawberry, *hêtre* = beech.
  human types – *garçon, héraut* = herald.
  words relating to **daily life** – *farder* = to apply make-up, *hache* = axe, *malle* = trunk, *gâter* = to spoil, *gravir* = to climb, *lécher* = to lick, *marcher* = to walk.
  parts of the body – *échine* = spine, *hanche* = hip.
  clothing – *gant, robe*.
  warfare – *guerre, flèche* = arrow, *blesser* = to wound.
- There are also a few **adjectives** – *frais, laid*, a number relating to **colour** – *blanc, bleu, brun, gris*, **adverbs** – *guère, (en) guise (de), trop*, and a **pronoun**, *maint* = many a, as well as a **prefix**, *mé-* and three **suffixes**, *-an* (as in *paysan*), *-ard* (as in *vieillard*) and *–aud* (as in *nigaud* = fool).

Latin

We must not allow ourselves to be over-impressed by the Gaulish and Frankish contributions to French, nor must we lose sight of the fact that the basis of modern French is Latin, Latin vocabulary and Latin grammar. Words that are unremarkable, words without which any sentence would be incomplete or would sound extremely awkward, are often words of Latin origin, essential but generally unassuming.

Classical Latin

The Latin with which we tend to be familiar, if we are familiar with it at all, is the Latin of the great writers and orators of Rome, known as **Classical Latin**.

This Latin was Latin at its best, perfectly correct in form, stylistically elegant, a model for all who wished to be noted in Roman society.

But it was not this Latin which formed the basis of modern French.

Exercise
Why did Classical Latin not form the basis of Modern French?

Vulgar Latin

The vast majority of the inhabitants of Rome and the Roman Empire spoke another variety of Latin, known as **Vulgar Latin**.

This Latin was derided and deprecated by those who spoke Classical Latin, as it departed from the norms of the former and had a flavour which was altogether different from it.

The speakers of Vulgar Latin
- **Vulgar Latin** was associated with the workers, the peasants, the ordinary citizens of the Empire, those whose lives were delimited by their need to survive, to find sufficient food, to have somewhere to live, the means of making a living.
- Such people were not concerned about the niceties that the users of Classical Latin discussed – they did not need abstract vocabulary or complex grammatical structures to discuss sophisticated philosophical matters.
- What they needed was a body of language which would enable them to cope with their everyday living.

Evidence of Vulgar Latin
- Evidence of this Latin of the ordinary people is to be found in a number of sources – not in the fine books and official inscriptions that were issued by the luminaries of Rome, but in the works of comic writers, who imitated the language of the ordinary people, in books on cookery, animal husbandry or medicine and also in scratchings on the walls of buildings, on oddments of pottery or on lowly tombstones, and also in lists of words proscribed as bad usage by the scholars of Rome.
- With no pretension to correctness or stylistic elegance, Vulgar Latin was the means whereby the masses of the population of the Roman Empire communicated amongst themselves.

Tendencies of Vulgar Latin 1
- Differences between Vulgar Latin and Classical Latin
   The major differences between the two varieties may be summed up as **simplification** and **regularisation** of complicated, irregular forms of the latter in the former.
   Many of the refinements and subtleties of Classical Latin disappeared from use in Vulgar Latin.
   The number of synonyms to express certain ideas were reduced.
   Irregular or highly synthetic constructions were regularised or made more analytical.

Exercises

Reduction of synonyms

The following words all meant 'beautiful' in Classical Latin. With your knowledge of modern French, which one or ones do you think may have been retained in Vulgar Latin? –

pulcher, bellus, formosus, venustus.

Similarly, which items from the following groups of words do you think survived in Vulgar Latin and were passed on into modern French? –

celer, rapidus, velox all = fast;

egens, nudus, indigens, indigus, orbus all = bereft, deprived.

Regularisation of irregular conjugations

- Verbs with the infinitival ending *-are* constituted the dominant verb class in Classical Latin and were conjugated in a regular manner.
- However, there were also many verbs which were irregular in their conjugations.

Examples

Irregular Classical Latin *canere* = to sing was replaced in Vulgar Latin by regular *cantare*.

In Classical Latin, irregular *ferre* = to carry had a near synonym in *portare* = to transport; Vulgar Latin speakers opted for the latter.

Classical Latin *edere*, also irregular, = to eat, but a slang word also existed, *manducare* = to chew, to chomp.

Similarly irregular *flere* = to weep was replaced by regular *plorare*.

Exercises

What are the benefits of adopting regularly conjugated verbs over maintaining irregular ones?

Can you guess what the Vulgar Latin forms, mentioned above, have become in Modern French?

Tendencies of Vulgar Latin 2

- **Derivation**

    Another tendency of Vulgar Latin was to create new words from already existing ones, especially by the process of derivation; in other words by adding prefixes and suffixes to words already in use (see Chapter 5).

    Sometimes this was done to give more substance to short words, at other times to avoid ambiguity (to distinguish words that sounded alike and might be confused), at others to indulge a liking for creating terms of endearment.

Examples of the use of diminutive suffixes

- Classical Latin *apis* = bee would have become just a single sound if the normal processes of phonological change had been followed (see below); to prevent the emergence of a minimal word (consisting of a single sound) with the attendant dangers of being missed in the course of speech and / or of homonymy, a derivative form, in this case a diminutive, was created; this form eventually > *abeille* (< *apicula*).
- In similar fashion *agnus* > *agneau* (< *agnellum*), *avis* > *oiseau* (< *avicellum*), *genu* > *genou* (< *genuculum*), *sol* > *soleil* (< *soliculum*).
- Slightly different circumstances dictated the development of *auris* > *oreille* (< *auricula*) – as a result of phonological changes (discussed below) *auris* was pronounced the same as *oris* = mouth, and was not too far distant from certain forms of the word = bone, *os (ossis)*; the scope for confusion was considerable, and the solution adopted was to create a diminutive form for *auris*, hence *auricula*.

The effect of Frankish speech habits on Vulgar Latin

- We have seen that a certain amount of Germanic / Frankish vocabulary has continued through into modern French.
- Frankish also had an effect upon the way in which the Gallo-Roman of Gaul was pronounced.
- The Franks' stress patterns were different from those used by the conquered population, and, as they learnt and spoke Gallo-Roman, they could not but impose their own patterns of usage. It was this that contributed considerably to the linguistic disruption of the Roman Empire and explains why French differs from the other languages which have descended from Latin, such as Italian, Portuguese and Spanish.

Unfortunately, given the nature of this book, it is impossible to trace and describe all the developments which took place in Vulgar Latin as the Franks influenced it. It is preferable to cast the net wider and attempt to give some insights into how Vulgar Latin became Modern French. As a consequence, we will ignore those developments which took place during the Old French (9th century to 13th century) and Middle French (14th century to 15th century) periods and deal with the beginning and end of the developments, the Vulgar Latin situation at one end and Modern French at the other.

1. Phonology – Sound Changes

It is very well claiming that French developed from Latin, but, in order to see how the various developments arose and why the modern French words differ in the way that they do from their Latin prototypes, it is necessary to know something of the 'laws' governing the phonological changes that took place in the formative period of the French language. Many centuries of development are going to be compressed in what follows, where we will attempt to bring out the major phonological trends that started in the Vulgar Latin spoken in Gaul and which eventually produced the modern French language.

Exercise

To give you the flavour of the processes that will be examined, a list of Latin words with their meanings follows. See if you can work out what the words have become in modern French –

canem = dog, *dormire* = to sleep, *hibernum* = winter, *mica* = crumb, *patrem* = father, *lactem* = milk, *florem* = flower

---

From the evidence contained in the above examples, it is possible to deduce some of the patterns of sound change which have caused Vulgar Latin to become modern French. But before you can do that, there are a few important facts that you need to know about the way in which the Latin language developed in the early centuries AD.

We will examine the fate of Latin vowels first and then that of consonants.

It is accepted that **phonology** does not appeal to everyone. You will be forgiven if you decide to proceed directly to **Word meanings** – but you will miss some fun!

The treatment of the vowels of Classical Latin in Vulgar Latin
- Classical Latin had **five basic vowels**, which could either be pronounced **long** or **short** (a distinction based upon quantity).
- These long or short **vowels were reorganised** in Vulgar Latin.
- The following factors governed sound change as Vulgar Latin evolved – (1) **quality** (the point of articulation of the vowel), (2) **stress** (how a word was accentuated) and (3) **neighbouring sounds** (which influenced the vowels in a variety of ways).

The effect of factor 1 – quality
- How qualitative considerations affected the long and short vowels of Classical Latin.
- Basically, the five Classical Latin vowels were paired together and reorganised to produce a pattern of seven vowels in Vulgar Latin.

  CL long i > VL [i]   CL short o > VL [ɔ]
  CL short i and long e > VL [e]   CL long o and short u > VL [o]
  CL short e > VL [ɛ]   CL long u > VL [u]
  CL long a and short a > VL [a]

The diphthongs of Classical Latin
- There were also three diphthongs in Classical Latin: æ, au, oe. They were eventually assimilated to the following vowels: æ > [ɛ], au > [ɔ], oe > [e].

The effect of factor 2 – stress
- The way in which words developed was greatly affected by how and where they were stressed. What follows accounts for most situations – we do not need to bother with uncommon ones.
- It is the vowel of a syllable that carries the stress.
- **Words consisting of a single syllable** are, of course, stressed on that syllable.
- **Words consisting of two syllables** are stressed on the first (penultimate) syllable. For **words consisting of three or more syllables**, if the vowel of the penultimate syllable is pronounced long, then that syllable carries the stress (an acute accent indicates the main stress) –
  e.g. *marítum = husband* > mari, *virtútem* = power > *vertu;*
- if that vowel is short (indicated by a grave accent), the main stress falls on the antepenultimate syllable –
  e.g. *árbòrem* > arbre, *ínsùla* > île.
- **Stressed syllables are retained in Modern French.**
- **Unstressed (weak) ones are generally not.**
  Tonic vowels bear the main stress, countertonic vowels secondary stress.

The effect of factor 3 – surrounding sounds
- It is usually the **consonants which follow the vowel** that determine its evolution.
- The most important possibility is whether the vowel occurs in what is known as a **closed or open syllable**, or in other words whether it is **blocked** or **free.**

Blocked vowel
  A vowel is blocked if it is followed by two or more consonants, except the following combinations, *bl, pl, br, dr, gr, pr, tr* which do not form a block.

Free vowel
  A vowel is free if it is in final position (i.e. nothing follows it), or is followed by another vowel, or is followed by a single consonant or one of the groups just mentioned.

Exercise
  Which of the vowels in bold in the following words are **blocked** and which are **free**? –

  arborem, duplum, labrum, locare, nasum, nodare, nutrire, portum, scriptum, villa.

  The Modern French descendants of these words are *arbre, double, lèvre, louer, nez, nouer, nourrir, port, écrit, ville.*

  Having identified whether the marked vowels are blocked or free and knowing what the words become in Modern French, you may now be able to deduce what the effect of blocking has on a vowel. Have you any thoughts on the matter?

Now that the three basic principles of phonology have been established – (1) that the vowels of Classical Latin were reorganised in Vulgar Latin, (2) that stress has a fundamental role to play in the subsequent development of Vulgar Latin vowels and (3) that whether a vowel is blocked or free also affects its development – it is time to examine what happens to the individual vowels.

> *A general principle regarding phonological development*
> - An important additional point to note regarding phonological change is that **provided that the same sound occurs in identical conditions, it always develops in the same way.**

1.1. The treatment of Vulgar Latin vowels

1.1.1. The treatment of stressed vowels

The following table brings together the three criteria mentioned above and shows how each vowel develops according to its phonological circumstances, with examples.

vowel	tonic		countertonic	
	blocked	free	blocked	free
VL [i]	> [i] tristem > triste villa > ville	> [i] ripa > rive vita > vie	> [i] civ(i)tatem* > cité lib(e)rare > livrer	> [i] hibernum > hiver privare > priver
VL [e]	> [ɛ] illa > elle mittere > mettre	> [wa] fidem > foi debet > doit	> [ɛ] circare > chercher firmare > fermer	> [ə] debere > devoir minare > mener
VL [ɛ]	> [ɛ] herba > herbe septem > sept	+ consonant > [ɛ] heri > hier petra > pierre + vowel > [je] sedet > sied	> [ɛ] mercedem > merci persona > personne	> [ə] fenestra > fenêtre nepotem > neveu
VL [a]	> [a] arborem > arbre caballum > cheval	+ consonant > [ɛ] mare > mer sal > sel + vowel > [e] nasum > nez	> [a] argentum > argent carbonem > charbon	> [a] amorem > amour maritum > mari
VL [ɔ]	> [ɔ] collum > col porta > porte	+ consonant > [œ] cor > cœur proba > preuve + vowel > [ø] potet > peut volet > veut	> [ɔ] dormire > dormir hospitalem > hôtel	> [u] colorem > couleur volere > vouloir

vowel	tonic		countertonic	
	blocked	free	blocked	free
VL [o]	> [u] cortem > cour rupta > route	+ consonant > [œ] florem > fleur hora > heure + vowel > [ø] nodum > noeud	> [u] subvenire > souve-nir turbulare > troubler	> [u] nodare > nouer subinde > souvent
VL [u]	> [y] nullum > nul purgat > purge	> [y] bruma > brume nudum > nu	> [y] jud(i)care > juger	> [y] fumare > fumer jurare > jurer

* Letters enclosed in brackets are weak vowels (see below) which disappear early, and therefore cause what was originally a free vowel to become blocked.

Exercise

Assign the following words to the appropriate cells in the table below, remembering that many of the words will have to be slotted in twice (once for the tonic and once for the countertonic vowels) –

amicum > ami, bibit > boit, clarum > clair, credere > croire, errare > errer, ferrum > fer, filum > fil, furorem > fureur, habere > avoir, lavare > laver, matrem > mère, me > moi, mortalem > mortel, novellum > nouveau, novem > neuf, pelare > peler, porcellum > pourceau, probare > prouver, servire > servir, soror > soeur.

vowel	tonic		countertonic	
	blocked	free	blocked	free
VL [i]				
VL [e]				
VL [ɛ]				
VL [a]				
VL [ɔ]				
VL [o]				
VL [u]				

Nasal vowels

Latin had no nasal vowels, but Modern French has four – so how and when did the nasal vowels of French come into being?

The history and origins of nasal vowels in French

- It seems that nasal *a* was the first to appear, in the 10th century, and the others were produced by the 13th.
- The process of **nasalising** vowels involved anticipating the pronunciation of a nasal consonant (*m, n*), by allowing air to pass through the nasal passages in advance of the pronunciation of the consonant, thereby giving a nasal quality to the vowel. Eventually the consonant was no longer pronounced at all.

The incidence of nasalisation

- Nasalisation occurs at the end of a word (after the loss of weak vowels and consonants), e.g. *bonum > bon*, and before a blocked nasal consonant, *m, n* followed by a non-nasal consonant, e.g. *campum > champ*.

The following table summarises the most significant developments:

vowel	tonic blocked	tonic final	countertonic blocked
VL / i / > /ɛ̃/	principem > prince quinque > cinq	finem > fin vinum > vin	prim(um) tempus > printemps
VL / e / > / ã / > / ɛ̃ /	prendere > prendre subinde > souvent	 plenum > plein sinum > sein	in fine > enfin vindicare > venger
VL / ɛ / > / ã / > / jɛ̃/	pendere > pendre ventum > vent	 bene > bien rem > rien	sentire > sentir tempestas > tempête
VL / a / > / ã / > / ɛ̃ /	campum > champ grandem > grand	 manum > main panem > pain	cambiare > changer mandare > mander
VL / ɔ / > / ɔ̃/	contra > contre longum > long	bonum > bon sonum > son	comp(u)tare > conter montanea > montagne
VL / o / > / ɔ̃ /	fundum > fond montum > mont	donum > don nomen > nom	contentum > content fundare > fonder
VL / u / > / œ̃ /		unum > un	lunae dies > lundi

Palatal sounds

The effect of surrounding palatal sounds

- The development of VL vowels was also affected by surrounding palatal sounds, the main ones being / k, g, dj, rj, tj / (the last three the result of *d, r, t* + following *i*, itself followed by another vowel (e.g. *diurnum > jour*)).

In the following table only those cases are given where a vowel develops differently from how it would if a palatal consonant were not in the vicinity. This is probably the most complicated aspect of Vulgar Latin phonology. Consequently, no offence will be taken if you decide to leapfrog over it.

palatal + VL / e /	tonic free / e / > / i / cera > cire mercedem > merci	
palatal + VL / a /		countertonic free / a / > / ǝ / caballum > cheval camisia > chemise
VL / e / + palatal		countertonic free / e / > / wa / legalem > loyal plicare > ployer
VL / ɛ / + palatal	tonic / ɛ / > / i / decem > dix legere > lire lectum > lit	countertonic / ɛ / > / wa / decanum > doyen sexaginta > soixante vectura > voiture
VL / a / + palatal	tonic / a / > / / (sometimes / e /) pacem > paix factum > fait	countertonic / a / > / ɛ / (sometimes / e /) laxare > laisser racemum > raisin
VL / ɔ / + palatal	tonic / ɔ / > / i / hodie > hui noctem > nuit	countertonic / ɔ / > / wa / focarium > foyer modiolum > moyeu
VL / o / + palatal	tonic / o / > / wa / crucem > croix vocem > voix	countertonic / o / > / wa / gloria > gloire potionem > poison
VL / u / + palatal	tonic / u / > i / ducere > duire fructum > fruit	countertonic / u / > / i / acutiare > aiguiser

Exercise

From the information set out in the above table, see if you can work out what the following Latin words have become in Modern French –

aquila, boscum, canalem, capillos, ecclesia, facere, jacere, medianum, nocere, octo, otiosum, pejor, rationem, regalem, sex, tectura, tractare, truite.

Exceptions

It may become apparent that a number of words do not conform to the patterns outlined above.

How exceptions occur
- In certain cases this is because of **assimilation or analogy**.

Examples of 'exceptions'
- *Amare* = 'to love' would normally become *amer* (in fact in Old French that was the form that is found); however, under the influence of other forms, formed regularly, beginning with *ai-* (for example the singular of the present indicative, *aim, aimes, aime* in Old French), the original form was adjusted to its present form (*amour, amant* perpetuate the original form).
- *Auscultare* = 'to listen' produced the form *asculter* in Old French, which on analogy with the large number of other words beginning with *es-*, was transformed into *escouter* and then *écouter* (see below).

1.1.2. The treatment of unstressed or weak vowels

Weak final vowels

The fate of weak final vowels
- Consider the following examples of Latin words and their modern outcomes –
  alba > aube, amat > aime, habere > avoir, murum > mur, muros > murs, sentire > sentir, venit > vient, viginti > vingt.
- It emerges that final *e, i, o, u* disappear, whereas *a* survives as *e* in spelling (originally pronounced).

Supporting vowels
- However, it happens quite frequently that in order to facilitate the pronunciation of the final consonant in the early language a supporting vowel was required –
  alterum > autre, insimul > ensemble (where a supporting consonant is also needed), *patrem > père, undecim > onze.*

Weak vowels within a word

Exercise

What happens in the following cases, where the vowel in question precedes the syllable carrying the main stress and is marked in bold? –

blasphemare > blâmer, bonitatem > bonté, collocare > coucher, dormitorium > dortoir, ornamentum > ornement, pergamenum > parchemin, simulare > sembler

and in the following cases, where the vowel occurs after the main stress but is not final? –

arborem > arbre, camera > chambre, purpura > pourpre, viridem > vert

Answer

  The situation is the same as with weak final vowels (preservation of *a* as an *e*; loss of the others).

1.2. Consonants

Vulgar Latin consonants are less liable to change than Vulgar Latin vowels. However, there are a few noteworthy cases where change does occur. It should also be noted that one or two consonants unknown in Latin emerge in French.

The incidence of consonants
  • Consonants occur in one of two positions, **strong** or **weak**.
    Strong position means that the consonant is in initial position, either of a word or a syllable.
    Weak position means that the consonant occurs between two vowels or that it closes a syllable before another syllable beginning with a consonant or that it is at the end of a word.

Exercise

  Indicate which consonants are in strong position and which in weak position in the following words –

    ardentem, caballum, carbonum, corona, donum, gustum, longum, privare, rupta, vita.

General principles regarding the fate of consonants
  • **Generally speaking consonants, whether single or in groups, in strong position remain the same in Modern French as in Latin.**
  • **Consonants in weak position change or disappear.**

In what follows some of the most significant developments will be recorded.

Consonants in initial position

The fate of consonants in initial position
  • As already stated, groups of consonants in initial position tend not to change, but groups beginning with an *s* are exceptions.
  • *s* in initial position disappears and is eventually replaced by *é* in Modern French.

Exercise

  What do the following Latin words become in Modern French? –

    · *scola* = school, *scribere* = to write, *scutum* = shield, *spatha* = spear, *sponsum* = spouse, *strictum* = narrow.

Consonants within a word

> *The fate of groups of consonants within a word*
> - Groups of consonants which do not occur in initial position in words tend to be reduced to a single consonant, usually the last one.
> - There are, however, a few exceptions:
>   when an *r* is involved, whatever its position, it remains intact;
>   the groups *fl, bl* also remain intact.

Exercise 1

What do the following Latin words become in Modern French? –

carbonem = coal, *fleb(i)lem* = weak, *inflare* = to inflate, *patrem* = father, *rupta* = road, *scriptum* = written, *servire* = to serve, *sufflare* = to blow, *viv(e)re* = to live.

Exercise 2

What happens to *s* + consonant in the following situations?

castellum = castle, *costa* = rib, *ess(e)re* = to be, *gustum* = taste, *piscare* = to fish, *spasmare* = to faint, *testa* = head, *vespa* = wasp.

- *The fate of c*
  Latin *c* / k / may stay as / k / or become / s / or / ʃ / depending on the following vowel: *c + a* > / ʃ /, *c + e, i* > / s /, *c + o, u* remains as / k /.
- *The fate of g*
  Similarly Latin *g* / g / has more than one outcome in Modern French: in addition to remaining / g /, it may become / ʒ / before the vowels *a, e, i.*

Examples

argentum = money, *gaudia* = joy, *genuculum* = knee, *gula* = throat, *gustare* = to taste, *gutta* = drop, *larga* = wide.

Exercise

What do the following Latin words become in Modern French? –

caballum = horse, *carum* = dear, *cantare* = to sing, *centum* = hundred, *cinerem* = ash, *cubitum* = elbow, *collum* = neck, *cor* = heart, *bucca* = mouth, *vacca* = cow, *peccatum* = sin, *porcellum* = piglet, *rad(i)cina* = root.

Consonants occurring between vowels

> *The fate of intervocalic consonants 1*
> - Consonants occurring between vowels, and therefore in a weak position, develop in a variety of ways, although a few remain the same in Modern French.
> - This is the case with *l, m, n, r, v.*

The fate of intervocalic consonants 2

- Amongst the most notable changes are *b* and *p* > / v /, *d* and *t* disappear. The
  situation with *c* is more complicated: sometimes it disappears, but sometimes
  it becomes / z / or / j /; that with *g* is the same as for *c*, but without the development of a / z /.

Consonants in final position

The fate of final consonants

- Final consonants also develop in a number of ways –
  m marking a noun ending disappears early – compare all the examples
  above and below.
  Other final consonants, marking the ending of the stem of the word, mostly
  disappear, but *p, v* became / f / and *l, r* stay the same.

1.3. New sounds and sounds that disappear

New sounds

- Sounds which did not exist in Latin are produced in the following circumstances – *b, d, p* and *v* + *i* followed by another vowel become / ʒ / or / ʃ /,
  depending on context.

- Other new sounds include / ɲ /, which results from the coalescing of *g* + *n*, *n* + *e* or *i* + another vowel.

Exercises

What do the following Latin words become in Modern French? –

diurnum = day, *jam* = now, *tibia* = stem, *sapiam* = may I know.

What do the following Latin words become in Modern French? –

agnellum = lamb, *montanea* = mountain, *signa* = sign, *unionem* = onion, *vinea* = vine.

A sound that disappears

- Conversely, Latin / h / does not survive into Modern French; consequently Latin words beginning with / h / produce words without / h / in French (but the *h* sometimes survives in spelling).

Exercise

What do the following Latin words become in Modern French? –

habere = to have, *herba* = grass, *hominem* = man, *homo* = one (pronoun), *hora* = hour.

The above information covers the most important developments which took place between the Latin and Modern French periods and should go a long way towards explaining the shape of many contemporary words and demonstrate their connections with their Latin prototypes.

2. Word meanings

It has been claimed that knowledge of Latin roots allows access to about 80% of contemporary French vocabulary. In what follows an attempt is made to provide a sample of the Latin contribution to French from a semantic perspective.

Popular and learned forms

- The distinction between Classical and Vulgar Latin has been well established earlier in this chapter.
- Another distinction needs to be introduced at this stage: the distinction between **popular** and **learned** forms.

Popular forms

This group comprises those forms which are the direct descendants of Vulgar Latin; they are forms which have gone through the various stages of sound change described above, with the result that often they seem to bear little resemblance to their Latin original.

Examples
> *aqua > eau, homo > on, coxa > cuisse*, and the list could be extended indefinitely.

Learned forms

The forms comprising this group have a quite different history.

They derive from Latin words which fell into disuse with the collapse of the Roman Empire, and which did not undergo the changes described earlier before entering French and the other Romance languages.

These words were subsequently resurrected several centuries later, when scholars in Europe began to rediscover the heritage of classical civilisation. These scholars often found that the vocabulary available in the Middle French period was not sufficient to convey the ideas and themes of the works produced by their classical predecessors a thousand years before. Consequently, in their eagerness to translate these works, they found themselves obliged to create new words, and to do this they regularly took as the basis for their new French words the Latin words for which they were seeking a translation.

The centuries of development which had acted upon the **popular** words and often rendered them unrecognisable in comparison with the Latin words they had been derived from, did not affect the **learned** forms.

These learned forms still bear a strong resemblance to the Latin words from which they have come.

Examples
> *deambulare > déambuler, femininus > féminin, patrimonium > patrimoine.*

Doublets

In a few cases the same Latin word may have both a popular and a learned descendant.

Doublets are the result of the same word, on the one hand, going through all the phonological changes involved in the process of Vulgar Latin gradually becoming Old French and then Modern French and thus producing a popular form, and on the other, being catapulted into reuse in the Middle French period and thus producing a learned form.

Examples of doublets 1 – doublets which are semantically connected
- In some cases the two French words are semantically connected.

Latin etymon	Popular descendant	Learned descendant
auscultare	écouter	ausculter = *to examine* (a patient)
fragilem	frêle	fragile
frigidem	froid	frigide
redemptionem	rançon = *ransom*	rédemption
sacramentum	serment = *oath*	sacrement

Examples of doublets 2 – doublets whose meanings have parted
- In other cases, the meanings have drifted apart.

Latin etymon	Popular descendant	Learned descendant
articulum	orteil = *big toe*	article
examen	essaim = *swarm*	examen
ministerium	métier	ministère
singularem	sanglier = *boar*	singulier

Many words retain the meaning they had in Latin in their subsequent forms in Modern French. The following is just a sample of elements from Latin – prefixes, suffixes and stems – which have produced words which have survived into Modern French and which more or less preserve their original meanings. The examples are divided into a number of categories.

Prefixes (see Chapter 5)

Examples of learned prefixes which continue to be productive in French

Prefix	Meaning	Examples
co-	together, with	coopérer, coprésentateur
ex-	out of	ex-dictateur, expatrier
in-	un-, in-	incroyable, incohérent
inter-	between	international, intervalle
pré-	before	préadolescent, prépayé
pro-	in favour of	proarabe, promonétaire
super-	over	superhygiénique, supermarché

▌ *Examples of popular prefixes which continue to be productive in French* ▌

Prefix	Meaning	Examples
dé- / dés-	parting	démanteler = *to dismantle,* désordre
entre-	reciprocity	s'entre-aider, entretenir
mal-	bad	malnutrition, malheureux
non-	denial	non-sens, non-violence
re-	repetition	regagner, renouvellement
sous-	beneath	sous-exposer, sous-marin
sur-	over	surestimation, surmener

▌ *Examples of other prefixes that are no longer productive* ▌

Prefix	Meaning	Examples
a- (also ac- / af- / al- / ap- / ar- / at- depending upon following consonant)	towards	amener, attirer
é- / ef-	out of	éconduire, effleurer
en- / em-	into	emmurer, enflammer
par-	through	parachever = *to complete fully,* parvenir
sou-	under	souligner, soulever
tré- / tres-	across	trébucher = *to fall over,* tressauter = *to jump*

Suffixes (see Chapter 5)

▌ *Examples of productive and non-productive suffixes* ▌

Productive suffixes	Examples	Non-productive suffixes	Examples
-able	confortable, rentable	-ade	boutade, promenade
-age	décryptage, voisinage	-ain	marocain
-aire	propriétaire, salutaire	-atoire	ostentatoire
-al	impérial, primordial	-elle	tourelle, tonnelle
-ance	abondance, croyance	-ie	bonhomie
-é	ailé	-if	poussif
-ement (forming nouns)	ornement, tutoiement	-ine	toxine

Productive suffixes	Examples	Non-productive suffixes	Examples
-eur	traiteur, tueur	-ise	franchise
-ité	spécialité	-itude	longitude
-ment (forming adverbs)	dramatiquement, éloquemment	-icule	monticule
-oir	grattoir	-ure	égratignure

Latin Roots in French

The number of roots from Latin which have contributed to the formation of modern French words is ... legion, and it is impossible in the scope of this book to do more than offer a hint of that enormous contribution. Consequently, only a brief selection of items is presented here, in the form of repeated patterns of transmission into modern French – reference to Bouffartigue and Delrieu (1981) and etymological dictionaries will give a fuller idea of the indebtedness of French to Latin roots. The purpose of this section is to allow you to obtain a picture of the all-pervasiveness of French words with Latin roots and how words that are seemingly unrelated etymologically may in fact be connected with each other.

Latin roots 1

- *Examples of elements of Latin words (not prefixes or suffixes) which may form the first or second part of a French word.*

Elements in initial position	Examples	Elements in final position	Examples
audio- = *hearing*	audiovisuel	-cide = *killing*	homicide
moto- = *moving*	motocyclette	-cole = *growing*	agricole
radio- = *radiation*	radiodiffusion	-lingue = *language spoken*	bilingue
socio- = *social*	sociolinguistique	-valent = *worth*	équivalent
vidéo- = *sending images*	vidéocassette	-vore = *devouring*	carnivore

Latin roots 2

- *Examples of French descendants of Latin root which reflect slightly different states of the root in Latin*

State 1 of root	French descendants	State 2 of root	French descendants
aestas	été	aestiv-	estival
agere	agir	act-	acte, acteur
facere / factus	faire / facteur	ficere / fect-	efficace / perfection
hospes	hôte	hospital-	hospital, hôtel
legere	lire	lect-	lecteur, lecture

State 1 of root	French descendants	State 2 of root	French descendants
mittere	mettre	-miss-	émission, permissif
scribere	écrire	-script-	descriptif, inscrire
vocitus	vide	vacu-	évacuer
videre	voir	-vis-	viser, visuel

Latin roots 3
- Example of a situation where a Latin root survives both as a root and as a suffixed form 1

  Latin *apis* = bee eventually became French *abeille* via the diminutive derivative form *apicula*. The consequence is that other modern French words descended from *apis*, like *apiculture*, do not bear a very close resemblance to *abeille*, although they all go back to the same Latin original term.

Latin roots 3
- Examples of situations where a Latin root survives both as a root and as a suffixed form 2

Original form	French descendants	Suffixed form	French decendant
avi-	aviculture	avicellus	oiseau
lucem / lumen	lucide, lumineux	luminaria	lumière
méd-	immédiat, médiéval	medianus	moyen
nov-	innover	novellus	nouveau
pisci-	pisciculture	piscionem	poisson
sol-	solaire, insolation	soliculus	soleil

Dual Origins of Words With Related Meanings

Sometimes words in modern French with related meanings but with different forms continue a situation which was current in Latin. A Latin word has as a rival another word, a synonym, and both provide descendants in modern French. The rival may be another normal Latin word or a more expressive, not to say vulgar, equivalent or a word from another language.

Examples of words with related meanings but different origins in Latin

Latin original	French descendants	Origin of replacement	Replacement	French descendant
os / oris = *mouth*	oral	CL	bucca = *cheeks*	bouche
pecunia = *wealth*	impécunieux	CL	argentum = *silver*	argent
puer = *child*	puéril	CL	infans = *infant*	enfant
rus / ruris = *countryside*	rural	CL	campania = *fields*	campagne
urbs = *town*	urbain	CL	ville = *farm*	ville

Latin original	French descendants	Origin of replacement	Replacement	French descendant
caput = head	décapiter, capital	vulgar	testa = jug	tête
cutis = skin (of humans)	cuticule	vulgar	pellis (skin of animals)	peau
equus = horse	équitation	vulgar	caballus = nag	cheval
edere / comestus (past participle of edere)	comestible	vulgar	manducare = to chew, to chomp	manger
lapis = stone	lapidaire*	Greek	petra = rock	pierre
loqui = to speak	locuteur, éloquent	Greek	parabolare = to use comparisons	parler
ambulare = to walk	déambuler, somnambule	Germanic	markon = to make a mark on the ground	marcher
bellum = war	belligérant	Germanic	werra = war	guerre
hortus = garden	horticulture	Germanic	gard = enclosure	jardin

Explanation of the meaning of lapidaire
lapidaire = brief, because stone-masons, engraving on stone, had to produce their work in as few words as possible.

One last pattern which affects a few modern French words concerns the way in which the declensional system of Latin has sometimes survived in French. Although it originally possessed a more complex case-system, during the Gallo-Roman period the Latin system was reduced to two cases (nominative, usually representing the subject and accusative, usually representing the direct object). In a few cases, both nominative and accusative forms of the same Latin word produce descendants in French which are different from each other.

> **Examples of words with different meanings deriving from different cases in Latin**

Nominative form	French descendant	Accusative form	French descendant
major = greater	maire	majorem	majeur
minor = smaller	moindre	minorem	mineur
homo = man	on	hominem	homme
senior = older	sire	seniorem	seigneur

Words That Change Their Meaning

Whereas it is often possible to define rules for the sound changes that turned Vulgar Latin into Modern French, the changes of meaning which also occurred are much less easily reducible to rules. What follows is an attempt to classify, through sets of examples, some typical semantic developments.

Linguistic conservatism

Linguistic conservatism

A situation where words stay more or less the same in form whereas their meanings evolve. **Linguistic conservatism** is a process which applies to many names of objects, ideas, institutions and scientific concepts. For example, there may be a continuity of technical or scientific or cultural development, but the words describing the products of the development do not change.

Examples
- Latin *carrus* (itself borrowed from Gaulish) originally referred to a four-wheeled wagon. Modern French *char* is a direct descendant of *carrus* but now describes a quite different type of vehicle (= tank).
- A modern *maison* is quite distinct from a Gallo-Roman *mansionem* = house, but the former word is the modern version of the latter.
- *Electricité* (created in the 18th century) is based upon the Latin word (of Greek origin) *electrum* = amber.

Specialisation or generalisation of usage (see Chapter 5)

Specialisation of usage

It happens quite regularly that words are taken from a general domain and used in a technical or specialised way in another. This has occurred with a series of words associated with farming: words of general application have been given new meanings when applied to farmyard activities.

Examples
Latin *cubare* = to lie down > French *couver* = to hatch; *mutare* = to change > *muer* = to moult; *trahere* = to pull > *traire* = to milk (before the invention of milking machines!).

Generalisation of meaning

The converse of specialisation of meaning also takes place, whereby a word from a technical or semi-technical domain is introduced into general usage, usually gaining a wider meaning in the process.

Examples
Latin *arripare* < *ad ripam* (a nautical term = to come to shore) > *arriver*, *nidacem* = nestling (i.e. a helpless young bird) > *niais* = stupid.

Change of range of meaning

Words may also broaden their meanings without necessarily passing from a special-ised to a general domain – the range of items or ideas covered increases or diminishes.

Examples
- **Extension** – French *oncle* continues Latin *avunculus*, which originally referred just to one's mother's brother, but because the corresponding noun for father's brother *patruus* fell into disuse, the former extended its meaning to cover that of the latter.
- The same applies to *tante*, which continues Latin *amita* = father's sister but assumes the meanings of *matertera* = mother's sister, which disappeared.
- **Restriction** – Latin *vivenda* = foodstuffs > *viande* = meat.

Euphemism (see Chapter 5)

Euphemism

People are sometimes reluctant 'to call a spade a spade' – it may be because the matter referred to is surrounded by superstition, associated with the supernat-ural, or is unpleasant or embarrassing in nature. The word which evokes the matter too directly is replaced by a **euphemism**, a less objectionable substitute. Eventually the substitute acquires the meaning and sometimes the force of the word it originally replaced.

Examples
- Latin *imbecillus* = weak, feeble was used in a euphemistic way to refer to someone weak in the head, mentally deficient; the Modern French descen-dant, *imbécile*, is no longer a euphemism and directly evokes such a person.
- In a similar way, Modern French *benêt* = silly derives from Latin *benedictus* = blessed (evoking the Beatitudes).
- From a different domain Latin *tutari* = to protect was used ironically in crim-inal circles to mean 'to take care of', 'to eliminate' > *tuer*.

Metaphor and Metonymy (see Chapter 5)

Metaphor

Latin words have regularly been drawn upon to provide a name for a new invention or discovery or simply to give a new name to something already in existence; in the process such words have undergone a change of meaning or have acquired a new meaning. At the root of many such developments is a **metaphorical association**.

Examples

- French *torpedo* derives ultimately from Latin *torpor* = numbness; a Latin derivative *torpedo* was used metaphorically to refer to the electric ray (fish), and when a new name was required to describe an underwater weapon, the Latin word was invested with a new meaning.
- The word *satellite*, which has applications in so many areas of modern life, derives from Latin *satelles* = life-guard, attendant.
- Metaphors have been drawn upon to name *parts of the body* –
  the shape of the muscle was compared to that of a small mouse; hence Latin *musculus* = small mouse > *muscle*;
  the head was likened to a jug; hence Latin *testa* = jug > *tête*;
  the shoulder to a spoon, thus *spatula* = type of spoon > *épaule*.
- They have also been called upon to give a *concrete value to an abstract idea* –
  Modern French *définir* may be traced back to Latin *finis* = end, limit;
  éliminer to *limen* = threshold;
  désirer to *sidus* = star.

Metonymy

Connected with metaphor is **metonymy**, the difference between the two phenomena being that the former is based upon a direct resemblance between two objects or an object and an idea, and the latter is based upon an association other than similarity between two objects or an object and an idea.

Examples

- Modern French *messe* = mass (in the Roman Catholic Church) comes from a phrase used at the end of the service – *ite, missa est* = go, the service is dismissed – where *missa* is the past participle of the verb *mittere* = to send, to dismiss, and was eventually applied to the whole of the service.
- French *témoin* = witness, a person who gives evidence, but derives from Latin *testimonium* = evidence; in other words the name of the person has displaced the activity originally conveyed by the noun.
- Similarly, *ivrogne* = drunkard derives from *ebrionia* = drunkenness.

Exercise

Try and discover the changes of meaning which the following words underwent in their passage from Latin to Modern French –

considérer, crétin, cuisse, finance, pondre, révéler.

Latin and Greek

Latin also served as the vehicle whereby a number of Greek words passed into French. Greek culture, literary, philosophical and scientific, held a profound fascination for the cultivated members of the Roman Empire. In addition Greek was used as the normal language for communication between groups speaking different languages in many Roman provinces of the eastern Mediterranean.

- Examples of common words –
  Common words taken over into Latin at this early time and which subsequently reached French include *beurre, bras, chaise, chambre, pierre*.
- Examples of specialised words –
  More specialised ones are *baume* = balsam, *girofle* = clove, *persil* = parsley, *trèfle* = clover.
- Examples of words relating to Christianity –
  An important group of specialised words of Greek origin, taken over into Latin, relate to the Christian Church, as Greek was the language of the New Testament and was used by the early Church in its liturgy.
  Words such as *ange, baptême, église, évêque, martyre, moine, prêtre* are typical products of this group.

Reference

Bouffartigue, J. and Delrieu, A-M. (1981) *Trésor des racines latines*. Paris: Belin.

Chapter 4

Words With a Foreign Origin

As stated in Chapter 3, despite the efforts of modern-day protectors of the French language to maintain its so-called purity, to eliminate or at least keep to a minimum undesirable foreign influences, French is in fact a lexical mongrel, made up of elements drawn from an enormous variety of sources. Any language is a mirror of its social, political, cultural and commercial history and none more so than French. Because French history has involved links with many other nations, foreign languages have made a notable contribution to modern French.

A number of issues need to be addressed before we can move on to an examination of the words of foreign origin in French.

The corpus
- It is necessary to define and delimit the corpus to be examined.
  Foreign words may be of two types.
  (1) Many of the foreign terms in French have become fully assimilated, an integral part of the language, in other words, they 'fit'. Indeed many of them go unnoticed.
  (2) Others, on the other hand, stand out as foreign imports. This is not of itself regrettable or reprehensible, as the purists would have us believe, but rather a sign of adaptability, of openness to the outside world, of healthy growth, a sign that French has risen to the challenge of a diverse world, which over the centuries has both increased in size and accessibility.
- Both types of foreign words need to be included in the corpus.

How do you define a French word?
- Answering this question raises a number of issues –
  What is French?
  Should we include all social varieties, informal as well as formal, all geographical varieties, those used outside metropolitan France as well as that / those used within?
  What period(s) should be considered?
  Many words common in the past are now archaisms: should they be included in a survey of modern French?
  How does a word qualify as French?
  How often does it have to be used?
  What status do foreign words occupy? etc.
  And when all is said and done, nothing stops any French person creating another neologism!

How many words of foreign origin are there in French?
- An indication of the number of foreign words in French may be obtained by referring to the introduction of the *Dictionnaire des mots d'origine étrangère* (1991).
- The dictionary suggests that 11.4% of French words are of foreign origin.

The problem of words that transit through a variety of languages
- Certain words of foreign origin do not pass **directly** into French – they pass into French not straight from the original language but by way of the **intermediary** of another language or other languages.

Example
>   In the case of *cimeterre* = scimitar, the original Persian form was *chamchêr*; in Turkish it became *chimchir*, in Italian *scimitarra*; it is this last word which accounts for the current French form, *cimeterre*.
>
>   Should French *cimeterre* be classed as of Persian, Turkish or Italian origin? – each language has had its contribution to make; the ultimate origin is Persian, the immediate donor is Italian.
>
>   In tracking the peregrinations and circuitous routes followed by certain lexical items, it is important to be aware of all the staging posts visited *en route* for French. In other words, it is not enough to be informed that such and such a word is Persian without at the same time being informed as to how that word arrived in standard French: all contributing languages need to be mentioned when the full history of a word is being recounted.

Dating
- Words that appear for the first time in a written or printed text may well have been circulating in the oral language for some considerable time. This is a particularly serious matter as far as early texts are concerned, since there is a gap of three hundred years or so between the emergence of French as an independent language and a sizeable body of literature recording it.
- In addition to the possibility of words being pre-literary, dating is beset with other hazards, since earlier instances of first appearances are discovered from time to time, and those that are recorded may simply be isolated examples, which bear little relation to the actual admission to the language.

Example
>   If *salir* is first attested in 1180, but *sale* only in the 13th century (Guiraud 30), what conclusions can be drawn? Three explanations are possible –
>   (1) Does that really mean that the derivative preceded the base form by at least a century? – a logical impossibility.
>   (2) Is *sale* to be considered a back-formation (i.e. derived) from *salir*? – unlikely.
>   (3) The most likely explanation is that *sale* predates *salir*, but was not recorded in any literature (or at least no example has yet been discovered).

- What complicates the picture still further is the fact that more important in the long run than the first attestation of a word is the time at which that word passes into everyday language and becomes current.

Examples

> *football,* first noted 1698, did not become current in French until the 19th century, nor *festin,* first noted 1382, until 1526 (Guiraud 8).
>
> Obviously the more recent the period under review, with fuller documentation being available, the more reliable dating becomes.

The Borrowing Process

Words enter French from a foreign source in one of three ways: they may be **brought in, fetched or sent**.

How words are brought into French

How words are brought into French 1

- As a result of **military invasion**.

Examples

> Most significant amongst early invaders were the Franks whose incursions and subsequent settlement in the country took place from the 4th century onwards (see Chapter 3).
>
> Other notable invaders were the Northmen (later known as Normans) in the 9th century and the Germans in the 20th century.

How words are brought into French 2

- As a result of **trade**.

Examples

> In the Middle Ages fairs were highly important commercial and social events, bringing together people not only from the immediate vicinity, but attracting traders from great distances – from Flanders and Italy in particular – and from closer to home – from other regions of France.
>
> Dutch and Italian words, and Arabic words via Italian, as well as dialectal terms were introduced into French in this way.
>
> During the later Middle Ages, Italians settled in France and established a rudimentary banking system, accounting for the fact that many French banking terms have an Italian origin.

How words are brought into French 3

- As a result of **royal patronage**, combined with cultural development.

Examples

> Marie de Champagne, daughter of Aliénor d'Aquitaine, attracted Provençal (Occitan) poets to her court in Champagne in a period spanning the 12th and 13th centuries.

Royal marriages between French and Spanish dignitaries also cemented relations between the two countries and facilitated the passage of vocabulary.

Particular technical skills offered by foreigners also account for groups of settlers being established and naturally making some linguistic contribution to the language of their host country: for example Dutch engineers assisted in draining certain marshy areas in the early 16th century, and a century later Dutch experts helped reorganise France's weaving, naval construction and hydraulic industries.

Words fetched into French

How words are fetched into French

- As a result of **exploration and tourism**.
  French explorers, adventurers or simply visitors, tourists visiting other lands report back on what they see and hear there.

Examples

They may see animals and plants that they have never witnessed before, topographical features which do not exist in their own country, domestic tools, buildings, means of transport, clothing which are distinctly foreign.

Voyages of discovery

- From the 16th century onwards European explorers were travelling to many parts of the world and discovering and bringing back to Europe new words for new objects. It is to the **Portuguese** and their journeys to the east, bringing back words from many languages spoken in Asia, and to the west, bringing back words from Brazil, and to the **Spanish** and their journeys to Central and Southern America and the Caribbean, that the French are indebted for the presence of words from these languages in their language.
- **English**, the language of the other great exploring nation, has provided French with words from North America, Africa and the East in particular.

Words are sent into French

How words are sent into French

- As a result of **ideas** which pass from nation to nation.
  The superior power of another nation's religion or philosophy may spur another nation to borrow words relating to these phenomena from the one where they originated or at least were largely practised and promulgated.
  Such words are transmitted by **scholars, missionaries, translators**.
  An intellectual channel is, therefore, the means whereby these words are spread from one language to another

Examples of how words are sent into French 1

- The Greek or Latin of medieval scholars has often provided the vital stepping-stone into French – Hebrew words relating to Judaism and Christianity arrived in French by that route many centuries ago.

- In the Middle Ages the intellectual superiority of the Arabs, in the domains of astronomy, mathematics, medicine and science in general, was so great that Arabic words were readily adopted by other scholars and transmitted from language to language.
- More recently other words from Arabic, this time relating to Islam, have arrived.
- Also, authors, wishing to add local colour to their texts, when they are describing foreign settings, in a sense choose foreign terms out of an **intellectual climate** which circulates in their environment.

Examples of how words are sent into French 2
- Peculiar to the 20th century is the **printed or electronic channel**.
- Words now speed from one language to another because of the power and efficiency of the media. At a time when mass communication is so omnipresent, rapid and simple to exploit, words are, as it were, introduced vicariously through the media, newspapers, magazines, radio, television, cinema, telephone, internet. Documentary programmes on the natural world, customs, habits, the way of life in other countries, fashion and entertainment often provide new words.
- Travelling is done via the airwaves rather than in person – direct human intervention in the transmission is no longer the main means for passing words from one language to another.

The processes combined – the case of English
- Nowadays all three processes may operate simultaneously.
- The all-pervasiveness of the influence of the **English** language in international affairs means that it is **brought** to France, and elsewhere, by visitors from the UK and the USA and the rest of the anglophone world
- English is **fetched** by French tourists who visit anglophone countries and come into contact with objects, customs and practices and probably also verbal expressions with which they were not previously familiar, who learn the vocabulary applicable to these matters and who then bring back with them the appropriate vocabulary. Perhaps even more obviously the influence of English is **sent out** from all directions, but especially from across the Atlantic Ocean, via the media in all their manifestations and the world wide web.
- The fact of being the world's leader in so many aspects of life has endowed the United States with tremendous prestige, with the corollary that English has acquired tremendous prestige too, so that using English words by non-English speakers becomes a mark of accomplishment and a means of enjoying reflected glory.

Reasons for Lexical Borrowing

Reasons why words are borrowed 1
- The most obvious reason is **gap-filling**.
  A gap becomes apparent when there is no equivalent in French for an object

or concept current in another language, and, rather than invent a new name for such an object or concept, speakers use the other language's term.

The types of words used to fill lexical gaps
- ### *Xenisms*
  Some terms have a relevance only to the country from which they originate – words describing specific topography, certain aspects of fauna and flora, buildings, social structure. These terms immediately evoke their country of origin and are known as **xenisms**, for example *ayatollah, escudo, kilt.*

The types of words used to fill lexical gaps
- ### *Words with no obvious cultural base*
  Such words become generalised, adopted as part of everyday speech and are used as if an integral part of the language.

The types of words used to fill lexical gaps
- ### *In-between words*
  Others words fall between the two previous extremes, in that although they still evoke their country of origin, they are also relevant in the country of adoption.

  Many recent American anglicisms relating to fast food and entertainment fit into this category – although such words may still have an American connotation, they have also become part of French society, and French speakers do not necessarily think of the USA when they use such terms.

Cultural prestige
- The purveyors of new words tend to belong to nations who possess high prestige. Prestige is to be counted in terms of economic, cultural, commercial, military might – countries possessing these in large measure exert enormous influence on others.

Examples
  Frankish during the early Middle Ages, Italian in the 16th century, American English in the 20th are all languages belonging to nations with high degrees of prestige.

Reasons why words are borrowed 2
- ### *Luxury borrowings*
  The matter of prestige also leads to the second major reason for adopting foreign terms: intellectual snobbery.

  These are **luxury borrowings**, borrowed unnecessarily, as a result of a desire to be trendy, to be considered well-informed and up-to-date. These terms are luxuries in the sense that there is already an adequate term available in French: it is just that the foreign term has desirable connotations which make it more attractive to the speaker than the conventional term.

  Such words are often resisted by the linguistic powers that be in France;

> *commissions de terminologie* consider them, and sometimes reject them, occasionally accept them as they are and occasionally accept them with a new nuance of meaning.

Foreign Borrowings in French

1. Celtic Languages

Early Celtic influences (Gaulish) have been discussed in Chapter 3.

1.1. Breton

Contact between French and Breton
- Refugees from Britain, dislodged by the dominant Anglo-Saxons, invaded France in the middle of the 5th century, settling in the north-west of the country and bringing their Celtic language, Breton, with them.

Examples
> The words of Breton origin in French are few and tend to preserve a **local flavour** –
> *biniou* = bagpipes, *dolmen, gallo, menhir*.
> Although *goéland* = seagull and *goémon* = seaweed do not specifically evoke Brittany, they are associated with coastal areas.
> The principal words with a general application are *baragouin* = nonsense, *bijou* = jewel, *cohue* = crowd, *mine* = appearance.

1.2 Celtic languages of the British Isles

Examples
> These languages are poorly represented in French, and what words from Celtic Britain there are tend to have been mediated by another language. From Gaelic come *slogan* (via English), *whisky*, from Irish *cloche* = bell, from Welsh *backgammon* (via English), *cromlech*.

2. Germanic Languages

2.1. Frankish

The Frankish contribution has already been discussed in Chapter 3.

2.2. German

Old High German / Middle High German
- **Old High German** (spoken between the 9th and 12th centuries) has contributed only a handful of words to French, e.g. *étoffe* = material, *sale* = dirty.
- The same applies to **Middle High German** (spoken between the 12th and 16th centuries) with, for example, *haillon* = rag, *blafard* = pale.

Contact between French and German
- The earliest recorded examples of **German** words in French date from the 12th century.
- It is from the 16th century that the number of German words entering French increased notably, and from the 19th that it increased really dramatically.
- The vast majority were borrowed directly into French (well over 90%).
- Others were mediated through English and occasionally French or German dialects.

The contribution of German-speaking mercenaries
- One or two words result from deformations of German expressions, brought to France by German-speaking mercenaries.

Examples
> *asticoter* = to polish < *dass dich Gott* (= may God . . . you), *bringue* = revelry < *(ich) bring (dir's)* (= cheers).

- These mercenaries, from Germany and Switzerland, were also responsible for the introduction of such words as *bivouac, cravate* = tie.

Types of borrowing (a small selection)
- *Calque*
  Croissant is a calque (translation, see Chapter 5) of *Hörnchen*, the name given to a pastry made to celebrate raising the siege of Vienna by the Turks in 1689 (the Crescent being the national symbol of the Turks).
- *Proper names*
  Place names, e.g. *berline* = saloon car.
  Personal names (usually inventors), e.g. *diesel, fuchsia, mach.*
  A name of nationality – *Croat > cravate.*

Semantic associations (a small selection)
- **Scientific, technical and intellectual terms**
  What is especially distinctive about the German lexical contribution to French from a semantic point of view is its scientific, technical and intellectual content.
- Many **inventions and discoveries** owe their French name to a German original.
  In the realm of **chemistry** *ester,* **physics** *diesel, ohm,* **vehicles** *taxi,* **anatomy** *plasma,* **geology or mineralogy** *cobalt, quartz, zinc,* **drugs** *héroïne, L.S.D.,* **medicine** *aspirine, gène,* **musical instruments** *accordéon, tuba,* from the **intellectual** sphere *introversion, paranoïa.*
  Warfare –
  From the Second World War in particular – **military** *obus, putsch,* and types of **buildings** *bivouac, bunker.*
  Economics and politics – *cartel, krach, diktat, national-socialisme.*
  Food and drink – *croissant, schnaps, vermouth.*
  Human types – *nazi, tsigane* = gipsy.

Domestic life, such as **clothing, domestic activities and objects** – *asticoter, album, bock* = beer glass, *cravate, robe*.
Sport and music – *handball, stand (de tir), lied, valse* = waltz.
Animals – *hamster, vampire*.
Plants – *edelweiss, fuchsia*.
One or two general words are less easily classifiable – *(se) blottir* = to curl up, *halte* = halt.

German as intermediary language

- German itself has been the means whereby a small number of words from other languages have reached French: from Czech *pistolet* = pistol, from Hungarian *coche* = stagecoach, from Swedish *nickel*.

2.3. Minority Germanic languages

Frisian

- The contribution from Frisian, spoken in present-day Netherlands and north-west Germany, is very small, the best known word being *savon* = soap.

Gothic

- Gothic – the Goths were an East Germanic tribe who had invaded southern and south-eastern Europe during the 2nd century AD – has only contributed a handful of words to French, principally *choisir* = to choose.

Semantic associations (a selection)

- Most of the words in this section have **human associations** –
  Human types – *bâtard* = bastard, *champion*.
  Appearance – *hagard* = dazed.
  Domestic objects – *banc* = bench, *harpe* = harp.
  Parts of buildings and collections of buildings – *beffroi* = belfrey, *bourg*.
  From the **inanimate world** come a small number of words –
  Colours – *blond, brun* = brown, **materials** – *ternir* = to tarnish, **topography** – *bois* = wood.

2.4. Scandinavian

Contact between French and Scandinavian

- From 838 onwards, the north and north-eastern coasts of France were invaded by Norsemen who even penetrated as far as Paris in 885. Present-day Normandy was ceded to them in 911.
- After a few generations the Norsemen / Normans abandoned their own language and adopted French, leaving behind a few linguistic traces.

Chronology and other characteristics of the Scandinavian contribution

- Three-quarters of the words of Scandinavian origin passed into French prior to the 17th century.

- The earliest recruits were *blémir* = to turn pale and *marsouin* = porpoise from the 11th century and the most recent *drakkar* from the 20th.
- Over half of the words have come directly into French, the others by a variety of routes.

Semantic associations (a selection)

- Terms with a **maritime** flavour predominate, from **collections of boats** – *flotte* = fleet, to **boats** – *drakkar*, to **parts of boats** – *tillac* = tiller, to **plants** – *varech* = kelp and **animals** – *eider*, *homard* = lobster, to **folklore** – *saga*, to **climatic conditions** – *banquise* = pack-ice.
- Other words relate less readily to the sea – *guichet* = counter, *bidon* = can, *duvet*, *regretter* = to be sorry, *joli* = pretty.

The contribution of individual Scandinavian languages

- Since the 17th century, individual Scandinavian languages have also made small contributions to the French lexicon, although in some cases the words are mediated by another language.
  From **Danish** – *narval* = narwhale.
  From **Icelandic** – *édredon* = eiderdown and *geyser* (from the name of such a spring in the south of the island).
  From **Swedish** – *dahlia* and *tungstène* = tungsten.
  Of the **Norwegian** words in French over half refer to **skiing**, including all the most recent borrowings – *slalom*, *ski*; the others refer to **animals** – *lemming* and *northern topograph* – *fjord*, *iceberg*.

2.5. Dutch

Contact between French and Dutch

- Words of Dutch origin have entered French at a fairly uniform rate since the 12th century, with a slight peak in the 17th century, but a marked decline in the 20th. Amongst the most recent borrowings is *apartheid*, evoking the presence of the Dutch (Boers) in South Africa.
- Relations between the Low Countries and France were especially close in the Middle Ages, as described earlier.

Dutch as intermediary

- Dutch has acted as intermediary for a number of words from other languages –
  From **Gaulish** – *dune*.
  From **Picard** – *cabaret*.
  From **Spanish** – *indigo*.
  And from much further afield – from **Malay** – *jonque* = junk.

Semantic associations

- The Dutch, like their northern Scandinavian neighbours, have contributed much in the way of maritime vocabulary.

- This all bears witness to the voyages of discovery and overseas trading undertaken by the Dutch, especially in the 16th century.
- This is to be seen not only in the lexicon of boats and sailing but also amongst the names of animals and elsewhere.

Examples of semantic associations (a selection)
- From the **maritime realm** – *flot* = wave, *flotter* = to float, *tribord* = starboard, as well as the names of various **fish** – *cabillaud* = cod, *crabe*, and **birds** – *pingouin*.
- Other **animals and plants** with less connection with the sea – *bélier* = ram, *pamplemousse* = grapefruit, *pomme de terre* (a calque modelled on a Dutch expression with the same meaning).
- A very large proportion of the Dutch words in French entail some **human association** –
  Human types – *mannequin* = model, *matelot* = sailor.
  Human activities, mainly **domestic** – *graver* = to engrave, *plaquer* = to veneer, *stopper* = to mend.
  Human characteristics – *drôle* = funny, *grommeler* = to grumble.
  Domestic objects – *bague* = ring, *drogue* = drug, *écran* = screen, items of **clothing** – *ruban*, **food and drink** – *bière* = beer, **buildings** – *brique* = brick, *cabaret*.
  Words describing the conventional **Dutch landscape** – *boulevard*, *digue* = dyke, *dune*.
  Human organisation – *loterie* = lottery, especially the world of **economics** – *action* = share, *boom*, *bourse* = stock exchange (the hotel of the Van der *Burse* family, decorated with three moneybags (*bourses*), became the home of the *Bourse* de Bruges).

2.6. English

The contribution of English to French has, of course, been enormous in recent years. Without entering into the debate of the rights and wrongs or the desirability or undesirability of this, this section examines those mainstream English words which have received approval by being recorded in the dictionaries. The *Dictionnaire des mots d'origine étrangère* cites just over 1000 anglicisms in French in the main body of the dictionary (and rejects an even larger number (1491 listed in the Appendix), as not being of mainstream usage). These are all words which are English in origin and which have passed directly from English into French. It was and still is normal for English words to pass directly into French. In addition to these direct borrowings, there are also a good many from other languages for which English has been the channel into French.

Contact between French and English
- From very small beginnings in the Old and Middle French periods, the break-through for English words came in the 17th century, with substantial development in the 18th century, and with massive growth in the subsequent two centuries. Almost half of the words recorded date from the 20th century.

- However, it is certain that many more English words have entered the language in the 20th century than are as yet recorded in the dictionaries.

The earliest English borrowings
  10th century – *pair* = peer;
  12th century – *bateau* = boat, *havre* = harbour and the names of the four cardinal points of the compass, *est, nord, ouest, sud* – the maritime flavour of these early borrowings from Anglo-Saxon is unmistakable.

Double entries
- A number of anglicisms have crossed the Channel twice, being French words which have passed into English, which have changed their meaning and / or form in some way in the latter language and which have then moved back to French with a new form and / or meaning.
- Sometimes the French word exists in its English form, sometimes the French form persists, with an additional meaning, in which case there has been a semantic rather than a lexical borrowing.

Examples *(a small selection)*
  auburn, bugle (bugle = ox; the English form is a truncation of *bugle-horn), cash* (*casse* = money-box), *confortable (conforter* = to uphold), *gadget* (perhaps < *gâchette), gay (gai), grapefruit (grappe), shopping (escope* = shop), *tennis* and *tennisman* = tennis player (*tenez,* exclamation used by server in what was originally known as *jeu de paume*)

Proper names *(a small selection)*
- Another plentiful source of anglicisms is proper names.
- From a semantic point of view, these words form a microcosm (albeit a large one) of the English contribution to French and to culture and science / technology in general – names associated with **plants, clothes, inventions, scientific discoveries, entertainment** all figure abundantly.
- The following types of names are involved –
  Personal names – *bloomer* (after the lady who started the fashion), *box-calf* (*Box* being the name of an English bootmaker), *jockey* (pet version of *Jock,* applied to grooms), *oscar* (perhaps ironic when used for an award).
  Place names – *jeans (Gênes), jersey, rugby, scotch* (whisky).
  Trade marks – *cellophane, formica, nylon, scotch* (sticky tape), *scrabble.*

Morphological considerations – types of anglicisms
- The major issue is the distinction between **genuine anglicisms** and **adapted anglicisms**.
- Just over half of the examples are genuine anglicisms, having exactly the same form in French as in English and just under a third adapted anglicisms.

Morphological considerations – adapted anglicisms
- In many cases the adaptation merely involves the addition of an accent, e.g. *acné, chèque, polaroïd.*

- In many other cases English affixes are given their corresponding French form, e.g. *agitateur, contraceptif, déodorant, sophistiqué, starlette.*
- Suffixation inevitably occurs when a verb is concerned, e.g. *disqualifier, dribbler.* Because of different pronunciation habits in the two languages, sometimes orthographic variation from the English occurs to facilitate acclimatisation into French – e.g. *biftek* = steak shows no *–s–* because of the French aversion for groups of three or more consonants, *moleskine* acquires an *–e* to avoid a final nasal vowel in French.

Exercise

How would you account for the spellings of *mildiou* = mildew, *poney, parquer?*

Morphological considerations – more extreme cases of adaptation and departure from the original term
- In other cases borrowings have departed a considerable morphological distance from their prototypes, especially as far as early borrowings are concerned – e.g. 14th century *dogue* < dog, 16th century *dériver* < to drive, *écraser* < to squash.
- A desire to gallicize English terms, especially polysyllabic words or those consisting of more than one semantic item, is seen in *boulingrin* = bowling green, *échiquier* = exchequer.
- More extreme still are cases where the English prototype has fallen into disuse – e.g. with *stylographe / stylo* the English term survived into the 20th century but is now no longer used.

Morphological considerations – double appearances
- In a number of cases, there are two forms in French for an anglicism.
- Often it is a question of a pure anglicism versus an adapted form or a deformation –
    e.g. *basket-ball – basket, fuel – fioul, jeans – jean, pull-over – pull, self-service – self.*

Morphological considerations – deformations
- **Deformations** are those words which have departed still further from their English originals – genuine English words have been truncated in some way –
    Sometimes by a single letter or sound – e.g. *brain-trust, short.*
    Sometimes by loss of a word in a multi-word item – *catch* < catch as catch can = wrestling, *goal* < goal-keeper, *golden* < golden delicious.

Morphological considerations – false anglicisms
- **False anglicisms** are items made up of English elements but which in fact are not genuine English words –

e.g. *baby-foot* = table football, *brushing* = blow-dry, *flipper* = machine game, *flipper* = to be affected by drugs, *footing* = jogging, *lifting* = face lift, *pressing* = dry-cleaning, *recordman* = record holder, *rugbyman* = rugby player.

- It should be noted that French seems to have acquired new suffixes in *-ing* and *-man* (equivalent to standard French *-age* and *-eur* / *-iste*).

Semantic considerations – calques

- **Calques** are **semantic loans**, that is the English meaning has been transferred to French words which translate literally the English word or add a new meaning, usually based on an English metaphor, to an already existing French word –

  e.g. *carotte* = incentive, *chemin de fer, gratte-ciel, haut-parleur, lune de miel, prêt-à-porter, soucoupe volante.*
  libre-service is a **semi-calque**, with one half translated, the other not.

Semantic considerations – discrepancy between English and French meanings

- Occasionally there is a semantic difference between the English and French words. **Extension of meaning** may be undergone in the French form –
  e.g. *palace* = luxury hotel
- Conversely there may be **restriction of meaning** in the French form –
  e.g. *dogue* = mastiff, *square* = public garden.
- A different meaning in French from English occurs with a few examples, involving *faux amis* –
  e.g. *chip* = crisp, *slip* = underpants.
- Finally, very occasionally **homonymy** is caused by the borrowing of two identical anglicisms –
  e.g. *scotch* = both adhesive tape and whisky.

English as intermediary (a small selection) 1

- Of course, not only has English supplied many words directly to French, but it has frequently acted as a conduit for words from other languages, some near to home, others from much further afield. In fact just as English has supplied more words directly to French than any other language, it has also mediated more than any other. From **Gaulish**, some with intriguing histories – e.g. *budget* which, with its original meaning, = leather bag, was borrowed into English, where it acquired its current meaning and which was subsequently taken over by French; similarly *tunnel* goes back to a Gaulish word = vat, becoming in Old French *tonnelle* = pipe, then arbour before passing to English and recrossing the Channel to France with its current meaning.

  From the territory of France, from **Normano-Picard** *acre, cottage,* and **Anglo-Norman** *haddock.*

  From Britain **Welsh** *backgammon* and **Gaelic** *clan, loch, plaid, slogan,* all of which denote typically Scottish traditions.

  From **Frankish** *bacon, hockey, standard, ticket.*

From **German** *dollar, gène.*

From **Scandinavian** languages e.g. from Icelandic *geyser*, from Norwegian *iceberg.* From **Dutch** *brandy, dock, doping, gin.*

From **Italian** *firme, investir, mascara, studio.*

From **Portuguese** *commando, vérandah.*

From **Spanish**, many with an American flavour – *alligator, banjo, cargo, marihuana, ranch.*

From **Arabic** *mohair*; but often in conjunction with another language, e.g. *albatross* through either Portuguese or Spanish before passing through English on the way to French; in a similar way *safari* passed through Swahili and then English before arriving in French.

Persian words likewise had complicated journeys before reaching English and then French – *châle* = shawl via Hindi, *pyjama* = pyjamas via Hindoustani, as did **Sanskrit** words – *jute* via Bengali, *tank* via Gujarati and Maratha, *punch* via Hindi, *jungle* via Hindoustani.

From **Chinese** *ketchup, kumquat,* as well as certain words of **Anglo-Chinese** pidgin origin (all 20th-century arrivals) – *chow-chow* a breed of dog, *pidgin* = pidgin language, *tchin-tchin* = cheers.

From **Maori** *kiwi,* both fruit and bird.

From **Polynesian** *tabou* = taboo, *tatouer* = to tattoo.

English as intermediary 2

* English is especially important for the transmission of words from the Indian subcontinent into French –

   From **Gujarati** *coolie,* from **Hindi** *bungalow, dinghy,* from **Hindoustani** *shampooing* = shampoo, from **Sinhalese** *atoll* (Maldives), from **Tamil** *catamaran, curry,* from **Tibetan** *polo.*

   From **Malay** *kapok* and *thé* = tea.

* Britain's colonising of Australasia brought a group of words of **Australian Aboriginal** origin into French, all reflecting indigenous fauna and customs –

   dingo, kangourou = kangaroo, *boomerang.*

   The Americas (see Spanish above) are also represented by certain **Amerindian** words, specifically from **Algonquin**; they refer in the main to North American phenomena: animals – *opossum, skunk,* Red Indians – *mocassin, totem,* transport across snow – *toboggan* and **Eskimo** – *kayak.*

   From South America, from **Arawak** (via Spanish) *canoë, mangrove.*

   From **Jamaican Creole** *reggae.*

The semantic classification of all the items borrowed from English into French would take many pages. What follows can be nothing more than a brief overview of the semantic areas involved. Examples will not be given, but can in most cases be found amongst those given in the linguistic classification.

Semantic associations 1

- Many words relate to **flora** and **fauna** and **topographical features** – many of the words are due to the colonising exploits of the British over a period of four hundred years and come from the four corners of the globe.
- It is **human life, endeavour, discovery and achievements** which account for much of the rest of the material. There are words relating to the **human anatomy,** to **health,** to **cosmetics**; those relating to **clothing and food and drink** again reflect the cosmopolitan flavour of English loan words, with words originating in the United States featuring quite significantly.
- The same can be said of the words relating to **buildings and parts of buildings**, where again there is a mixture of home-produced items as well as others from more far-flung environments.
- There are many words concerning **objects, utensils and pieces of equipment** relating to **domestic and business activities**; many of these words have a modern, often electronic, ring.
- The realm of **invention** covers a very wide range of objects, going from the paraphernalia associated with the **military and transport** to the concepts of **chemistry and astrophysics.** Linked with invention are the names of a quite large number of **materials** which have been discovered or invented in the English-speaking world, including **textiles** and other domestic or commercial materials. There are also many words with an **intellectual** value, involving the **social sciences, linguistics, philosophy, economics, politics,** the latter being a particularly large contributing area.

Semantic associations 2

- **Human types** figure prominently amongst the words denoting humans in general, sometimes because they denote a type which is typically or originally British or American or because anglophone speakers gave a name to this type of individual before anyone else: there are words with a **political, professional, sporting, religious or philosophical** connotation, other indicating an **evaluation**, to be admired or deprecated, or an **age-group** or marking a position in an **hierarchy.**
- The **sporting life** has of course spawned a very large number of terms relating to various sports, most of which originated on British soil, although there is a smattering of American items as well: amongst these are names of **sports, organisations and competitiveness and the tactics** involved.
- It is in fact the world of **entertainment,** in which of course sport plays an important part, that has caused many anglicisms to be adopted by French. There are words relating to **games, music and dance crazes, musical instruments, the theatre and shows of various types, books, magazines and journalism, travel and holidays.**
- From the more shady side of life come terms concerning **drugs and crime.**
- On the more personal level, there are many words denoting **human characteristics and states of mind.**

- Mankind's attempts to organise the world and put their stamp upon it are crystallised in many of the anglicisms of French – for example the names of **measurements, currency and cash, business and its conduct, legal terms, care of products and marketing**.
- **Communication** has become exceedingly important and complex in recent years, and this is reflected in the large number of anglicisms related to it, with **publishing and the mass media** being extremely significant. **Meetings** and their conduct also make their contribution.
- Both pleasant and unpleasant aspects of **human relations** figure, as do names of **nationality and languages, social groups, folklore**.
- In addition there are many terms whose meanings are either extremely **general** and apply in many areas or so vague that they cannot be tied down to one particular area.

3. Romance Languages

3.1. Occitan

Contact between French and Occitan
- Since they share very close geographical proximity, being spoken on the same national territory, it is not surprising that there have been many borrowings into French from Occitan.
- It is customary nowadays to use the term *Occitan* rather than *Provençal* to refer to the collection of southern dialects known historically under the title *langue d'oc*; strictly speaking Provençal is simply one of these dialects (albeit the most prestigious, historically at least).
- Occitan words have passed into French in considerable numbers during the whole of its history with peaks in the 16th and 19th centuries. Each of these two centuries saw an Occitan renaissance take place. Another peak occurred in the 17th century.
- The first direct borrowings took place in the 11th century – *olive, port* = mountain pass; the latest ones, from the 20th century, include *fada* = stupid, *pétanque, pissaladière* = fish salad.

Occitan as intermediary language
- As is to be expected, the vast majority of Occitan borrowings, having their roots in French soil, passed directly into French.
- A few were mediated by other languages or dialects.
- On the other hand, Occitan has served as the intermediary for many words on their journey into French – from **Arabic** *luth* = lute, from **Frankish** *garer* = to park, from **Hebrew** *canne* = cane, from **Italian** *anchois* = anchovy, from **Sanskrit** *muscade* = nutmeg, from **Spanish** *soubresaut* = somersault.

Semantic associations (a small selection)

- Quite a high proportion of the words of Occitan origin in French relate to the **natural world**, very often that of the Occitan area itself: names of **plants**, especially **fruit and vegetables** – *brugnon* = nectarine, *figue, piment* = pepper, names of **animals** – *abeille* = bee, *aigle* = eagle, *tortue* = tortoise, words relating to **climate** – *brume* = haze, *mistral*, to topography – *brousse* = scrub-land, *cap* = headland, to **regional dishes** – *aïoli, bouillabaisse*, to **local buildings** – *auberge* = inn, *mas* = Provençal farmhouse.

- Associations with the **sea** are also prominent – *cargaison* = cargo, *chavirer* = to capsize.

- Another large proportion of the Occitan words in French relate to the **human sphere**: words denoting **human types** – *cambrioleur* = burglar, *troubadour*, **clothing** – *foulard* = scarf, **domestic activities** – *biner* = to hoe, **domestic objects** – *cadeau* (which has undergone an interesting succession of associated meanings: from Latin *caput* = head, to chief, to capital letter (13th century), to decorative lettering, to superfluous words (17th century), to entertainment offered to a lady (17th century) to its current meaning (end 18th century)), *casserole, flûte*, **human activities** – *railler* = to mock, *rôder* = to prowl, **human characteristics** – *ébouriffé* = dishevelled, *jaloux* = jealous.

3.2. Italian

Contact between French and Italian

- Italian has been supplying French with new words since the 12th century, and in very large numbers since the 14th, doubling in numbers between the 14th and 15th centuries and quadrupling in the 16th, which represents the zenith in Italian borrowings. It was of course at this time that a vogue for things Italian, including military matters, the arts, science, intellectual and daily affairs, swept France. The number of borrowings was halved in the 17th century with a gradual reduction in the 18th and 19th, followed by a relatively small number coming across into French in the 20th.

- However, it should be noted that, after English, Italian remains the most generous lexical contributor to French.

- Amongst the first words of Italian origin to be found in French were *cape* and *perle* = pearl.

- The 20th-century borrowings relate mainly to food – *cannelloni, pizza*, politics – *fascisme* = fascism, 20th-century discoveries (or lack of same!) – *analphabétisme* = illiteracy, *marina, pizzeria*.

Italian as intermediary (a small selection)

- Italian itself has served as an intermediary language in a large number of cases, the majority of which arrived in French during the heyday of Italian influence, the 16th century. The languages involved are particularly European, but also include some from further east.

- From within **Europe** – from **Gaulish** *brio*, from **Frankish** *groupe*, from **Longobardic** *balcon* = balcony, from **Basque** *bizarre* (the word itself has had an appropriately unusual semantic history: from Basque *bizar* = beard, then = energetic man, to Spanish *bizarro* = bold, to Italian *bizarro* = hot-headed, to its current meaning).
- From further afield (and many of the terms came to French from Italian only after being mediated through one or more other languages) – from **Arabic** (a large number of words are involved) *coton* = cotton, *zéro*, from **Persian** *bronze*, *douane* = customs, from **Sanskrit** *riz* = rice, from **Turkish** *caviar*.

Proper names (a small selection)
- A particular feature of Italian influence is that a considerable number of common nouns in French owe their origin to Italian proper names.
- Personal names – *pantalon* = trousers (Venetian actor, Pantaleone), *volcan* = volcano (Vulcan).
- Place names – *charlatan* (an inhabitant of Cerreto, famous for its peddlers of medicines and indulgences), *galerie* = gallery (Galilee, the name given to a church porch where, like Galileans at the time of Christ, people came to hear the word of God), *gorgonzola* (Italian town).

Semantic associations (a small selection)
- The **natural world: animals** – *calmar* = squid (originally = writing desk; the change of meaning was occasioned through the association between the liquid secreted by squids and the ink used at such desks), *guépard* = cheetah, *perroquet* = parrot; **plant** names comprise **trees, flowers, fruit, vegetables and spices** – *brocoli* = broccoli, *chou-fleur* = cauliflower (a calque), *citrouille* = pumpkin, *lavande* = lavender, *mandarine, orange*; **climate** – *rafale* = gust, and **topography** – *cascade* = waterfall, *piste* = track, *plage* = beach.
- **Humans** are represented by their **anatomy** – *torse* = torso and especially their **clothing**, with Italian influence in the area of **fashion** being particularly striking – *costume* = suit, *veste* = jacket, *parfum* = perfume. Related to clothing are a number of names of **fabrics** as well as of other types of **materials**, a number of which are associated with volcanoes – *brocart* = brocade, *faïence* = earthenware, *lave* = lava. **Human types** themselves account for a large proportion of the Italian words in French, from the cowardly to the brave, from the young to the old, from the clergy to the military, from the lowly to the most exalted – *altesse* = highness, *assassin, ballerine* = ballerina, *caporal* = corporal, *capucin* = Capuchin (friar), *partisan, soldat* = soldier.
- These human types are accompanied by a similarly wide range of **human attributes and characteristics**, going from *altier* = haughty to *caprice* to *fougue* = enthusiasm, to *politesse* = politeness to *svelte* = slim.

Semantic associations 2
- **Human activity** is well represented, again with a vary wide range of meanings, from *accaparer* = to hoard to *caresser* = to caress to *fracasser* = to smash to

trajet = journey, as are the objects associated with such activities – *balle* = ball, *carton* = cardboard, *médaille* = medal, *valise* = suitcase.

- Italian influence can also be seen in a number of other areas of human existence, the **organisation of society** – *agence* = agency, *camp, police* = policy, *vogue* = fashion, **maritime**, concerning in particular the structure of the boat and its lading – *escale* = port of call, *proue* = prow, *remorquer* = to tow, and **military matters** – the military terms have the flavour of battle about them, consisting of names of weapons, summonses to war, battle formations and so on – *alarme* = alarm (originally a cry to arms), *bataillon* = batallion, *bombe* = bomb, *canon* = cannon.
- Linked to these terms are some from the realm of **transport** – *ferroviaire* = railway, *frégate* = frigate, *gondole* = gondola.

Semantic associations 3 – culture and economics

- The lexis of Italian origin in French is pervaded by a sophisticated, cultured atmosphere, reflecting in particular the progress made by Italy in the realm of the arts and finance in the 16th and 17th centuries. This is the really original part of the Italian contribution to French. Most of these words were borrowed between the 16th and 18th centuries.
- The **artistic side** covers a wide range of activities: words from **architecture** – *balustrade, colonnade,* from **painting** – *aquarelle* = water-colour, *dessiner* = to draw, from **dance** – *ballet, entrechat,* from **literature** – *nouvelle* = short story, *sonnet,* **theatre** – *burlesque, intermède* = interlude, names of **buildings** with Italian prototypes, and where Italian concepts and designs are often clearly evident – *casino, citadelle* = citadel, *vestibule* = hall.
- Of course many **musical** terms have been borrowed from Italian, most of which relate to the style in which a piece of music is to be played, a few of which are names of musical instruments (many of the terms have an identical form in English) – *adagio, air, mandoline* = mandolin, *mezzo-soprano, violon* = violin.
- Italy's contribution to **economics** is seen in such words as *banque* = bank, *bilan* = balance sheet, *solde* = balance.
- In more recent times, Italian **cooking** has contributed a wide menu of terms to French – *caviar, semoule* = semolina, *tagiatelli* (see also the beginning of the section).
- A handful of terms defy classification, mainly because of their very **general** application. Most common amongst them are *briller* = to shine, *calme* = calm, *chiffre* = number (originally from Arabic), *risque* = risk.

3.3. Portuguese

Contact between French and Portuguese

- Portuguese words first appeared in French in the 15th century, and a few have entered the language in each century since that time, with nearly half arriving in the 17th, the century of major Portuguese colonial expansion.

- The first Portuguese word recorded is *caravelle* = boat; the most recent demonstrate the linguistic importance of **Brazilian Portuguese** in the 20th century – *bossa nova, favela* = slum.

Portuguese as intermediary (a small selection)

- Portugal's sea-faring reputation from the late 15th century onwards is reflected in many words reaching French via Portuguese from many parts of the world. In fact more words have passed from more distant countries into French via Portuguese than from Portugal itself. Portuguese influence in the east accounts for words from Arabic, Persian, Sanskrit, various Indian languages, Malay, Chinese and Japanese.

  From **Arabic** *mousson* = monsoon.

  From **Persian** via Hindi *bazar* = bazaar.

  The **Indian subcontinent** has also supplied a number of terms via Portuguese – from Sanskrit via Tamil *pagode* = pagoda, from Tamil *mangue* = mango.

  From **Malay** *bambou* = bamboo.

  From further east Portuguese has channelled words from **Chinese** *cangue* = shackle and **Japanese** *bonze* = Buddhist priest or monk into French.

  From **Africa** – from Bantu *banane* = banana.

  From the **Tupi-Guarani** language of Brazil *acajou* = mahogany, *ananas* = pineapple.

Semantic associations (a small selection)

- From a semantic point of view no one category figures particularly prominently amongst the mainstream Portuguese terms in French. However, if all the words, from whatever source, whether they are pure Portuguese or adopted from some other language, are taken as a whole, the most striking feature is their **exotic** flavour, the result of Portugal's colonial achievements.
- In the words from Tupi-Guarani, **flora and fauna** are very conspicuous; in those from the east it is **plants** which dominate, with a few names of **human types**.
- Words arriving in French directly from Portuguese are marked by a (P).

  From all sources there are a number of words relating to **human types** – *albinos* (P), *mandarin, nègre* (P) and **human activities,** involving **entertainment,** e.g. **dances** – *bossa nova* (P), *samba* and a **song** *fado* (P) and **trade** – *bazar.*

  Human organisation – *caste* (P), *fétiche* (P) = fetish, *paria*, **coins** *cruzado* (P), *roupie.*

  Food and drink – *marmelade* (P), *sangria.*

  The names of **buildings** with a Portuguese origin evoke Portugal's colonial exploits – *case* = hut (P), *favela* (P), *pagode*, as do the words denoting **transport** – *jonque*, and those denoting **meteorological phenomena** – *mousson, typhon.*

  Animals and plants with Portuguese names similarly recall Portugal's past: **animals** – *cobra* (P), *jaguar, piranha, zèbre* (P), **plants** – *ananas, bambou, banane.*

3.4. Spanish

Contact between French and Spanish 1
- Contacts between France and Spain are of long-standing and of many types, geographical, cultural, political, religious as well as personal.
- Historically speaking, there is only a sprinkling of Spanish terms in French dating from before the 16th century. Amongst the earliest words attested are *cuirasse* = breast-plate from the 13th century and *baie* = bay, *épagneul* = spaniel from the 14th.

Contact between French and Spanish 2
- Thereafter words from Spanish have entered the language in fairly copious numbers, with peaks in the 17th and 19th centuries, each accounting for about one quarter of the words.
- The most recent terms are very diverse, including food and drink – *paella, xérès* = sherry, entertainment, often with an American (both north and south) flavour – *canasta, rodéo, rumba,* especially bull-fighting terminology – *toréer* = to be a bull-fighter and 20th-century values – *machisme, macho.*
- A distinction amongst these 20th-century terms can be drawn between those Spanish borrowings of European origin and those from the Americas.
- From the Americas come such words as *cañon, macho,* more specifically *lasso, tango* from Argentina, *rumba* from Cuba, *marihuana* from Mexico.

Spanish as intermediary 1
- The majority of Spanish borrowings have passed directly into French. However, a relatively small number of Spanish words have been mediated by other languages: Old French, Dutch, Italian and especially English and Occitan.
- On the other hand Spanish itself has acted as an intermediary for a large volume of words from other European languages and beyond, reflecting various aspects of the contacts which the Spanish have had firstly with neighbouring and then with more distant nations.
- Some such words originated amongst the early **Iberian** tribes, who came from Africa, in about the 6th century BC and occupied the south-west area of present-day France as far north as the Loire – *baraque* = hut, *carapace* = shell.
- Spanish has also channelled a small number of other words of fairly ancient origin into French: from **Celtic** *silo,* from **Frankish** *estampille* = stamp.
- It has acted in the same way for another group of words, this time from Latin and the Romance languages: from **Latin** *embargo, vanille* = vanilla, from **Occitan** *romance,* from **Italian** *volcan,* from **Portuguese** *créole, embarrasser* = to embarrass.

Spanish as intermediary 2 – Arabic (a small selection)

- The invasion of Spain by the Arabs in the early 8th century and the subsequent five centuries-long occupation by them made the Spaniards the vehicle for the dissemination of Arabic culture and the Arabic language in western Europe.
- A number of words of Arabic origin owe their presence in French to Spanish intervention – *rame* = ream (of paper), *récif* = reef, *tabac* = tobacco.
- Arabic was also the staging-post for a number of other words from the languages of neighbouring countries which passed into French after a stop-over in Spanish and sometimes in another language: from **Turkish** *gilet* = waistcoat, from **Berber** *sagaie* = assegai, from **Persian** *sarabande* = saraband.
- Very circuitous was the route followed by *aubergine*, from Sanskrit via Persian and Arabic before being taken over into Catalan and then on to French.

Spanish as intermediary 3

- In the case of a few other words of eastern origin, Portuguese was the original contact language, from which Spanish subsequently borrowed them before passing them on to French, e.g. Sanskrit *carambolage* eventually = cannon in billiards and traffic pileup (the original term denoted an exotic red fruit) began its lexical journey via Marathi (a language spoken in western India) before reaching Portuguese.

Proper names

- Place names – *épagneul* (Spanish), *gitan* = gipsy (Egyptian), *havane* = cigar (Havana, Cuba), *mayonnaise* (Mahon, Menorca, to celebrate the capture of the town by the duc de Richelieu).
- Personal names – *véronique* (named after Saint Veronica, the sweeping gesture of the torero resembling that of the saint, wiping Christ's face)
- Trade mark – *gomina* = hair cream.

Semantic associations (a small selection)

- Semantically speaking, the words of Spanish origin in French and those mediated by Spanish fall into well-defined categories and often clearly evoke their Spanish origin. Those words with an Arabic origin are denoted by (Ar) after the word.
- **Human types** – *camarade* = friend, *gitan* = gypsy, *guérillero* = guerilla, *nègre* = negro.
- Rather surprisingly there are no parts of the human anatomy with a Spanish name, whereas a number of **human qualities and characteristics** have – *brave, embarrasser, macho, svelte*.
- **Human activities**, among which **entertainment** figures very strongly, **dancing** – *flamenco, rumba, tango,* **bull-fighting** – *corrida* = bullfight, **card-games** – *canasta,* **chess** – *case* = compartment (originally referring to the squares on a chessboard), and **dicing** – *hasard* (Ar) = chance; more **general** words are *palabre* = palaver, *sieste*.

- **Intellectual** words, related to **orthography** – *cédille* = cedilla and **literature** – *romance*.
- **Human organisation** – **coins** – *peso*, **language** – *sabir* = lingua franca, **political activities** – *démarcation* (a word created by Pope Alexander VI in 1493 to separate Portuguese East Indies from Spanish West Indies), *firme* = firm and **interpersonal relationships** – *compliment*.
- **Domestic objects** (both European and South American) – **musical instruments** – *castagnettes, guitare* (Ar), **tools** – *lasso, machete*, **cosmetics** – *gomina* = hair cream; *carafe* (Ar), *rame* (Ar) = ream (of paper).
- **Buildings** – *alcove* (Ar), *mosquée* (Ar) = mosque, *patio*.
- **Clothing, food and drink** – **clothing** – *casque* = helmet, *gabardine, sombrero*; **food** – *caramel, mayonnaise, pastille* = pastille.
- **Smoking** also owes much of its vocabulary to Spanish influence – *cigare, havane, tabac* (Ar).

Semantic associations 2

- **Maritime transport** and associated activities: **boats** – *embarcation* = small boat, *flottille* = flotilla, **parts of a boat** – *misaine* = foresail, **equipment** – *embarcadère* = landing stage, **trade** – *embargo* (originally used in shipping).
- The **military** contribution is much smaller – *guérilla* = guerilla warfare.
- The **animal** kingdom is well represented – *albatross* (Ar), *bourrique* = donkey, *canari* = canary, *épagneul* = spaniel, *moustique* = mosquito.
- Most of the words which derive from Spanish relating to **flora and topography** in general not only betray their origin but also evoke the voyages of discovery and subsequent exploration associated with the Spanish from the 16th century onwards – **plants** – *abricot* (Ar) = apricot, *jonquille* = daffodil, **topography** – *baie* = bay, *volcan* = volcano.
- Names of **materials and minerals** – *jade, satin* (Ar) (named after the Arabic version of the Chinese town name where satin was produced).
- **Climate** – *rafale, tornade* = tornado.

Spain and the New World

- Another major factor in the Spanish contribution to French was its New World maritime and colonial adventures starting in the 16th century. As a result Spanish became the vehicle whereby many words from Central and South America and the Caribbean reached France, particularly words from **Arawak** (spoken in Latin America and the Caribbean), **Carib** (spoken in the Caribbean and Guyana), **Nahuatl** (spoken in Mexico) and **Quechua** (spoken in Peru).

Examples (a selection)

All the words clearly evoke **local conditions and phenomena**.

Arawak – *canoë* = canoe, *hamac* = hammock, *iguane* = iguana, *maïs* = maize and *ouragan* = hurricane.

Carib – *caïman* = cayman, *cannibale* = cannibal, *pirogue* = dugout.

Nahuatl – *mescaline* = mescaline (derived from an agave), *ocelot*, types of plants – *cacao* = cocoa, *chocolat, haricot* = bean, *tomate* = tomato.
Quechua – the names of animals figure large – *condor, lama* = llama, *puma*; also *gaucho* and *caoutchouc* = rubber.

4. Dialects of French and the Regional Languages of France

4.1. Dialects

4.1.1. Southern dialects

Examples 1 (a selection)
None of the southern dialects has supplied more than a handful of words to French.
Gascon – *cèpe* = boletus, *cagnotte* = kitty, *traquenard* = trap (originally it described the way a horse trots, then a trap for trapping animals before acquiring its figurative sense), *tôle* = sheet metal.
Languedocien – *palombe* = woodpigeon, *banquette* = seat.
Béarnais – *béret, bagarre* = fighting.
Savoyard – *grèbe* = grebe, *crétin*.
Examples 2
Lyonnais (the largest contribution from the southern dialects but still relatively small). Many of the most recent borrowings have a somewhat derogatory or low register connotation – *bafouiller* = to splutter, *frangin* = brother, *jacasser* = to chatter, *moutard* = brat.
* Borrowings from other dialects tend to involve obscure or esoteric meanings.

4.1.2. Northern dialects

Examples
The contribution of the northern dialects is considerably greater than that of the southern dialects, and some of the items show distinctive **northern associations**.
Walloon – **mining** terms figures prominently – *faille* = fissure, *houille* = coal, *rescapé* = survivor.
Picard – also some mining terms – *coron* = miner's house, *porion* = miner, but also common terms – *figer* = to fix, *cabine* = cabin, *gribouiller* = to scribble.
Normano-Picard – *accabler* = to overwhelm, *cabrer* = to rear up, *colimaçon* = snail, *crevette* = prawn.
Norman (the largest contingent of terms) – *car* = coach, *cassette* = casket, *éclair* = flash, *s'enliser* = to sink in. *Vaudeville* takes its name from the Norman village of Vau-de-Vire, famous for its musical entertainments.
Norman as *intermediary* – from Gaulish *quai* = embankment, from Frankish *ricaner* = to grin, from Germanic *houle* = swell, from Scandinavian *crique* = creek.
Anglo-Norman – *pieuvre* = octopus.

> Northern words of unspecified origin – *usine* = factory. Most have an informal ring – *taule* = bedroom, *toqué* = crazy.

- These dialects also *mediated* a number of words – from Gaulish *boue* = mud, from Frankish *danser* = to dance, from Dutch *dégingandé* = awkward.
- The lexical atmosphere created by the words borrowed from northern dialects is qualitatively different from that created by those from the south: industrialisation, factories and mines are apparent in the former rather than foodstuffs and topographical features. What is also interesting is that human types and characteristics with northern names express either a humble or an undesirable social position – *maquereau* = pimp, *saligaud* = bastard, nor are the nouns describing the human form particularly flattering – *caboche* = head, *cloque* = blister, *mafflu* = heavy-jowled.

4.1.3. Western dialects

Semantic associations 1

- The contribution of the western dialects is about a third of that of the northern dialects.
- There is quite often an atmosphere of disreputableness similar to that pervading many of the northern terms. This is especially seen in the names of human types – *dupe* (based on the name of the *huppe* = hoopoe, 'a notoriously stupid bird'!), *filou* = crook and words expressing human characteristics, e.g. *billeversées* = nonsense, *s'engouer* = to have a craze, *fâcher* = to annoy.

Semantic associations 2

- Words with a **domestic** connotation – *lessive* = washing, *pichet* = small jug.
- The **climate** of the west of France and its effects – *bruine* = drizzle, *noroît* = northwesterly wind, *gadoue* = mud.
- **Seafaring preoccupations** of its population in the past – *bernicle* = limpet, *chaloupe* = trawler.
- **Plants** – *aubépine* hawthorn, *cassis* = blackcurrant, and perhaps surprisingly *liane* = creeper (from the Caribbean) which recalls the voyages of discovery made from the west coast.

4.1.4. Central and eastern dialects

Examples

> The contribution from these areas is very small indeed.
> **Central** area – *poussière* = dust, *rillette* = potted meat.
> **Eastern** area – *beurre* = butter, *oie* = goose, *ronchonner* = to grumble.

4.2. The regional languages

Of the regional languages, it is **Occitan** which has supplied by far the largest number of words to French – see Section 3.1 – with **Breton** a very poor second – see Section 1.1. The other regional languages have contributed little and what there is generally evokes the appropriate region.

Examples
> **Alsatian** words tend to have a **culinary** association – *choucroute* = sauerkraut, *quiche, riesling.*
> For **Basque** it is pelote – *pelotari* = pelote player.
> For **Corsican** the local vegetation and related activities – *maquis, vendetta.*
> For **Flemish** – *kermesse* = fair.

4.3. French outside France

As with the regional languages, words from Francophonia tend to evoke local phenomena and are consequently quite esoteric.

Examples
> From **Louisiana** – *cajun.*
> From **Caribbean creole** – *biguine, zombi.*

5. Hamito-Semitic languages

5.1. Arabic

Contact between French and Arabic
* A large majority of the words of Arabic origin in French arrived via other languages. Arabic lexical influence reached its zenith in the 16th century when Arabic influence in so many areas of culture was also at its highest. About quarter of the Arabic terms in French entered the language at that time. A resurgence occurred in the 19th century, largely as a result of renewed interest in North Africa and the beginnings of colonialisation by French and other European settlers.

Early and late examples
* The earliest Arabic word to be used in French was *amiral* = admiral.
* The 20th-century terms document the re-emergence of Islam as a world force, with such words as *ayatollah, fedayin* = fedayee, *moudjahid, ramdam* = ramadam, and a renewed interest in the Arab way of life, especially food-stuffs, such as *merguez* = sausage.

Arabic as mediated and intermediary language
* Many of the earlier arrivals were mediated by other languages. In fact only just over a third of the Arabic words arrived directly in French – most of these referred to specifically Arab phenomena, Islam and religious practice and Arab customs and civilisation.
* Of the major contributors to French, Arabic is the language which has seen its words follow the most diverse of routes into the receiver language.
* The major intermediary languages, accounting mainly for terms of a less localised nature, were Italian, Latin, Spanish.
* Arabic has been instrumental in mediating words from the Middle East to French.

- From **Persian** *tasse* = cup, but more often Arabic figures in combination with a European language in the mediation of Persian words into French – *azur* = blue, *douane* = customs, *échecs* = chess, *épinard* = spinach, *jasmin* = jasmine, *sucre* = sugar.

Proper names

Personal name – *ottomane* = ottoman (furniture).

Place names – *fez*, *mousseline* = muslin, *oasis*.

Béni-oui-oui = yes-man is a hybrid, consisting of Arabic *béni* = son of + reduplication of French *oui*.

Semantic associations

- The vast majority of the words clearly evoke the **Arab world**.

Human types – these provide an intimate summary of the structure of Arab society – *ayatollah, bédouin, cheik* = sheik, *chiite* = Shiite, *musulman* = Muslim, *toubib* = doctor.

Human characteristics – *maboul* = crazy; **human activities** – *masser* = to massage and *nouba* = spree (originally designating an Algerian military band).

Islam – *Coran* = Koran, *islam, ramadan*.

Domestic objects – *divan, tasse,* **cosmetics** – *khôl* = kohl, **clothing** – *caftan, djellaba, fez,* **food and drink** – *couscous, élixir, merguez,* **buildings** – *harem, médina, souk*.

Military terms – *baroud* = fight, *matraque* = club, *razzia* = raid.

Scientific or technical terms – *alcali* = alkali, *azimut* = azimuth (a bearing in astronomy).

Fate – *baraka, nadir, zénith*.

Natural world: animals – *gazelle,* **plants** – *haschisch, henné* = henna, *moka* = mocha, **topography** – *bled* = rolling countryside, *erg* = dune.

Materials – *laiton* = brass, *ouate* = cotton-wool.

5.2. Hebrew

Semantic associations

- The early borrowings from Hebrew, usually via Latin and / or Greek, tend to have a **Christian** connotation, the later ones a **Jewish / Israeli** one, but on the whole it is Christian terms that are the most notable from a semantic point of view – *alléluia, amen, Pâques* = Easter, *sabbat* = sabbath.
- In addition there are some examples of **calques**, all of which have a Christian connotation – *ange* (Hebrew *mal'ak* = messenger > Greek *aggelos* = messenger, then Latin *angelos*), *calvaire* = calvary (Hebrew *golgotha* = place of the skull > Latin *calvariae locus*).
- General words – *canne* = cane, *cidre* = cider, *sac* = bag.
- German accounted for two borrowings – *sémitique* = Semitic, *yod*.
- The earliest Hebrew borrowing in French is *chérubin* from the 11th century and the latest *kibboutz* from the 20th.

5.3. Persian

Contact between French and Persian
- A relatively large number of words of Persian origin have been borrowed into French, most having been mediated by other languages.
- Although Persian words from all sources have entered French in all centuries, the summit was reached in the 15th and 16th.

Persian as a mediated language
- Most Persian words arrived in French after a circuitous journey, often involving more than one intermediary language.

    A single language: **Arabic** *tasse* = cup, **Italian** *bronze*, **Latin** *pêche* = peach, *persienne* = blind, **Turkish** *kiosque* = kiosk.

    Two languages were involved in the following cases: **Arabic and Italian** *douane* = customs, **Arabic and Latin** *épinard* = spinach, **Greek and Latin** *paradis* = paradise, **Hindi and English** *tigre* = tiger, **Hindi and Portuguese** *bazar* = bazaar, **Hindoustani and English** *pyjama* = pyjamas, **Turkish and Italian** *turban* = turban.

    The place name *pârs* = Persia is involved in *pêche*, *pers* = sea-green, *perse* = Persian, *persienne*.

5.4. Sanskrit

Contact between French and Sanskrit
- There has been a steady flow into French of words from Sanskrit since the 12th century, with a notable increase in the 19th century, and, as with Persian, only a few, and most of these of recent date, have arrived in French direct from Sanskrit. The others have had complicated journeys, with quite often three earlier ports of call (*sucre* = sugar boasts five!).

Sanskrit as a mediated language (a selection)
- **Persian and Arabic** are the common denominators in a certain number of cases, together with **Greek and Italian** for *cramoisi* = crimson, with **Greek and Latin** for *muguet* = lily of the valley, with **Greek, Latin and Italian** for *sucre*, with **Latin** for *nénuphar* = waterlily, *poivre* = pepper, with **Italian** for *orange* = orange (*orange* arrived in French from Italian where it had the form *arancia*; the French town Orange, being famous for the sale of such fruit, exerted phonetic influence upon its form, hence *orange*); **Persian, Greek, Latin and Italian** provided *riz* = rice.
- Quite often an Indian language is involved: **Bengali and English** for *jute*, **Hindi and English** for *punch*, **Hindi, English and Portuguese** for *sangria*, **Hindoustani and English** for *jungle*.
- Words that have arrived directly in French often have a religious association, whether through philosophy – *nirvana*, *svastika* = swastika, *yoga*, *zen*, or through the names of practitioners – *gourou* = guru, *yogi*.

5.5. Turkish

Examples of Turkish as a mediated and intermediary language
- Only a few words of Turkish origin have entered French directly – *chagrin* = leather, *yaourt* / *yoghourt*.
- Various languages have acted as intermediaries for other words – **Italian** *caviar*, **Arabic and Spanish** *gilet* = waistcoat.
- Turkish itself has been the means whereby a number of **Persian** words in particular have gained access to French – *kiosque, tulipe, turban*.

5.6. Various other Hamito-Semitic languages

Mediated languages and semantic associations
- The words from these languages in French tend, as might be expected, to be mediated by other languages (usually Arabic, Greek or Latin) and to have a **local** flavour.
    Egyptian *ébène* = ebony, *oasis, pharaon* = pharaoh.
    Syriac *damas* = damask (from Damascus).
- However, the **Aramaic** terms in French have a **religious** connotation – Judaistic *rabbin* = rabbi, Judaeo-Christian *messie* = messiah, Roman Catholic *abbé* = abbot.

6. Other languages

Many other languages have made a smaller contribution to French. They are listed below by continent rather than language group.

6.1. Africa

Contact between French and African languages
- African words began to appear in French from the 16th century onwards.
    The first such word was *gri-gri* / *gris-gris* = amulet (of Ewe-Fon origin).
Examples
    From the **Bantu** group (the largest contribution) – *chimpanzé* = chimpanzee, *tsé-tsé*.
    From **Malgasy** – *raphia* = raffia.
- Mediation
    Some words have passed direct into French. Others have been mediated by European languages, especially Portuguese and English –
    Via **Portuguese** *banane* = banana, *macaque*.
    Via **English** *okapi, mandrill*.
- Semantic associations
    African flora and fauna are strongly reflected in the borrowings.

6.2. Asia

Chinese
- Linguistic contacts with **China** date back to the 16th century, the earliest direct borrowing being *litchi / letchi* = lychee.
- A fair proportion of the words of Chinese origin have been mediated by other languages, especially **English**, e.g. *ketchup, kumquat.*
- The vast majority of the words relate directly to China or the **Chinese way of life**.

Japanese
- Most of the **Japanese** words in French arrived in the 19th and 20th centuries.
- Semantic associations
    As with the Chinese borrowings, they reflect many of the **customs** and especially the **martial practices** of their society.
    Martial arts – *jiu-jitsu, judo, karaté*, with words for types of suicide, *hara-kiri, kamikase* and another denoting the samourais' code of honour *bushido.*
    Drink and clothing – *kimono, saki.*
    Professions – *geisha, mikado, samouraï.*

The Indian subcontinent and Tibet
- Words from the **Indian subcontinent** and **Tibet** entered French in relatively large numbers in the 17th and 19th centuries. Over half the words have been mediated by a European language before reaching French, principally **English**.
- *Semantic associations*
    Most of the words involved have precise values, many evoking specifically **Indian phenomena**, such as the names of local **animals** – *panda, zébu*, names of **materials** or **clothing** – *calicot, sari* and **human types** – *dalaï-lama, sherpa.*

Indonesian and Malay
- The East – **Indonesia** and **Malaya** – was of considerable interest and importance to travellers particularly between the 16th and 18th centuries, and this is reflected not only in the semantic fields represented by the borrowings but also by the number of European nations which have channelled words into French – Dutch, English, Portuguese, Spanish.
    Names of **animals** predominate – *émeu* = emu, *orang-utan.*

6.3. Australasia

Australasia
- Words from **Australia** and **New Zealand** have usually been mediated by **English** and have a strong **local** flavour.

Aboriginal *dingo, kangourou* = kangaroo, *boomerang.*
Maori *kiwi* = kiwi, both fruit and bird.
Polynesia *tabou* = taboo, *tatouer* = to tattoo and *bikini* (a trade name derived from the name of an atoll).

6.4. Europe (in addition to contributions from languages discussed in earlier sections)

Northern and Central European languages
- In comparison with the Scandinavian contribution, dealt with earlier, that from other **northern European** languages is very small.
  Baltic area – *élan* = eland; **Finnish** *sauna*, **Lapp** *toundra* = tundra.
  Central Europe –
  Czech *pistolet* = pistol, *robot*; **Hungarian** *paprika, goulache / goulasche* = goulash; **Polish** *polka, meringue.*

Russian
- The largest contribution, with examples dating back to the 15th century.
- The largest contingent arrived in the 20th century and has a distinctly **Soviet and post-Soviet** flavour – *goulag, soviet, glasnost, perestroïka, rouble.*
- Some of the words relating to **human types** reflect the **pre-Soviet** period – *cosaque, tsar*. The **Russian way of life** is illustrated by such words as *datcha, balalaïka, samovar, icône* = icon, *steppe.*

6.5. America

6.5.1. North America (in addition to those words from North American English, dealt with in Section 3.10.)

Amerindian languages
- A very small contribution.
  Algonquin *caribou*, **Choctaw** *bayou* and **Iroquois** *séquoia.*
  Eskimo *igloo, anorak.*

6.5.2. South America

Mediated languages
- **Spanish** has been the intermediary language for the following South American languages – **Arawak**, spoken in Latin America and the Caribbean, **Carib**, spoken in the Caribbean and Guyana, **Nahuatl**, spoken in Mexico, **Quechua**, spoken in Peru (see Section 4.4).
- **Portuguese** has mediated a sizeable proportion of the relatively large number of **Tupi-Guarani** words in French. Most of the words refer to animals – *toucan, tapir.*

7. Summary – The Major Contributors

Certain languages have emerged as particularly influential in determining the shape of modern French. The most notable languages in this respect are, in decreasing numerical importance, English, Italian, Occitan, Spanish and Frankish. The links between the nations using these languages and French are clear. Historically the fortunes of these nations and France have been closely intertwined. The fate of Occitan, spoken on French soil, has been dictated by political decisions made in Paris. Rivalry and occasionally co-operation mark the relationships between the other nations and France. In the case of English, French was a net contributor to the developing language from the 12th century and for a number of centuries thereafter. The tables were not turned in that relationship until the 18th century, when English became a very serious factor in enlarging the French lexicon with terms from many areas of contemporary life. English and French belong to different linguistic families – Germanic as opposed to Romance. In the case of two of the other contributing languages mentioned above, Italian and Spanish (and the same also applies to Portuguese, ranked 10 amongst contributing languages), what they have in common with French is membership of the same linguistic family. This definitely facilitates movement between the languages, as there are fewer structural barriers to overcome – words from such origins are more easily assimilated into French than words from unrelated languages. Not only are there strong historical links between all these major contributory languages and French, but closely connected to that is the fact that they are also close geographically, their land masses in some cases being contiguous to each other, and with only a narrow stretch of water separating the English-speaking domain from France.

This principle of geographical proximity would also account for the relatively large impact which the various dialects of France have had upon the standard language. Speakers of French dialects and also the regional languages, of which Occitan is one, have been or still are to a greater or lesser extent bilingual, which would make passing of words from the former into the latter more easy.

The following table presents the languages in descending order of importance of contribution to French (down to a contribution of 1% and excluding pre-Indo-European and Gaulish).

The figures speak for themselves: as is well known, English is the largest contributor of loanwords to French, accounting for almost a third of the total and surpassing its nearest rival, Italian, by over 10%. Italian accounts for one fifth of the total, and then there is an even larger drop to the third and fourth ranks, Occitan (8%) and Spanish (7%). Thereafter other languages and the French dialects come pell-mell.

References

Dictionnaire des mots d'origine étrangère, compiled by Henriette and Gérard Walter (1991). Paris: Larousse.

Guiraud, P. (1965) *Les Mots étrangers*. Paris: Presses Universitaires de Paris.

Rank	Name of language	Proportion of contribution (%)
1	English	30.5
2	Italian	20
3	Occitan	8
4	Spanish	7
5	Frankish	5
6	Northern dialects	4.5
7	German	3.5
8	Dutch	3
9	Arabic	2.5
10	Portuguese	2
11	Southern dialects	2
12	Western dialects	1.5
13	Germanic	1
14	Scandinavian	1
15	Russian	1

Chapter 5

Words with a Short History – Neologisms

The French vocabulary is changing constantly, undergoing a permanent process of renewal. Words drop out of use – consulting dictionaries of earlier periods will soon confirm this.

Exercise

Which of the following are likely to have disappeared from use and are unlikely to be still recorded in a dictionary of contemporary French? Why?

balance des paiements = balance of payments
besanter = to decorate with besants (coins from Byzantium)
congé de maternité = maternity leave
coût-efficacité = cost-effectiveness
festage = tax paid to lord when ridge-piece of roof laid
gonfanon = pennant attached to a lance
se guimpler = to put on a wimple
joste = joust
missile de croisière = cruise missile
pull = pullover

But more importantly new words – neologisms – are being constantly produced. These fall into three major categories –

(1) **Borrowings from other languages.**

(2) **Internal creations** – words made from elements already existing in French.

(3) **Changes of meaning** of already existing French words.

Neologism

For our purposes neologisms are those words which have entered French, by whatever means, over the past fifty years, in other words since the middle of the 20th century.

Caveat 1
- Only some of the words created every year will become permanent features of the language, but it is a risky business trying to predict which ones will survive and which will disappear.
- Obviously those which are tied to a particular event, which was significant at the time but which soon fades into obscurity, or an individual's name, that of

a star or politician who occupied centre stage for a short period but who was soon forgotten or replaced by another star or politician, are the least likely to find their way into dictionaries.

Examples

> *Do you remember Edouard Balladur from whose name, during his period of political influence, the term* balladurien *was derived, or Raymond Barre who, during his, donated* barriste?

Caveat 2

- Even those new words which do eventually find a permanent slot for themselves in the language do not have an easy time of it, and are regularly criticised by members of the *Académie française* as ugly or unnecessary.
- However, to their chagrin, it is not the Academicians who decide the fate of new words, but ordinary speakers, and especially the trend-setters of the time.

Exercise

Suggest who the trend-setters of the second half of the 20th century have been and who they are likely to be in the 21st.

The need for neologisms

- On the whole, neologisms serve two main purposes –
  firstly, **to fill a gap** in the lexicon
  and secondly, **to embellish** the language, to provide a different way of expressing something.
- See Chapter 4.

Exercises

What sort of gaps are likely to appear in a language's lexicon?
Why are 'luxury' items needed?

Foreign borrowings – these have been dealt with in Chapter 4.

Internal Creations

The most important types of new words encountered under this heading are derivatives, compounds, shortenings. It should be noted that derivation has always been a source of new words for French; composition less often, and word shortening was relatively rare before the 20th century. In what follows we shall concentrate mainly upon words that have entered French since the second half of the 20th century.

Derivation

> **Derivation**
>
> The simplest way to create a new word in French is to add an affix, either a prefix or a suffix to one which already exists.
>
> Derivation is a process which is convenient, neat, economical and usually unambiguous.

Prefixation

> **Prefixation**
>
> Prefixes are elements which are appended to the beginning of an already existing word.
>
> Normally the prefix cannot stand by itself, although one or two prefixes have gained word status as a result of ellipsis or word-shortening, e.g. *super, télé.*

Prefixes may be divided into a number of categories according to their meanings.

Prefixes denoting opposition

- The 20th century having been a century of change, revolutions, reversals, inventions, there has been a great need for prefixes to form antonyms to express the opposite of what is denoted by the original term.

  Examples

  The most common prefixes of this type are –

  — *anti, contre, dé, in, non.*

  anti – examples – *des phares anti-éblouissants* = anti-dazzle, *une loi anti-grève, un médicament anti-stress, une politique anti-européenne.*

  contre – examples – *des mesures contre-ingérence* = counter-insurgency, *une contre-offensive, une contre-culture.*

  dé – examples – *déforester, la dépénalisation des stupéfiant* = decriminalisation, *le déstockage d'une entreprise* = off-loading of stock, *se désaltérer* = to quench one's thirst

  in (*in* becomes *il, im, ir* before *l, m, r* respectively) – examples – *ininfluençable* = uninfluencable, *l'illiquidité* = lack of liquidity, *irrelié* = unconnected, *imbiodégradable* = unbiodegradable (note the two prefixes).

  non – examples – *la non-agression, la non-prolifération des armes nucléaires, le non-remplacement des départs* = natural wastage.

Prefixes denoting degree

- Not only is the 20th century a century of radical change, it is also a century of superlatives – the biggest, the smallest, the strongest, the fastest, in short, the best.
- This is reflected in the host of prefixes suggesting some type of degree.

Examples
   Prefixes denoting a high degree –
   archi, méga, super, sur, ultra
   archi – examples – *archicomble* = full to bursting, *archi-faux* = utterly wrong, *archiplat* = extremely dull.
   mega – examples – *une méga-pôle* = mega-city, *une mégatournée* = mega-tour.
   super – examples – *superchouette* = absolutely brilliant, *supersophistiqué, un supermouchard* = supergrass.
   sur – examples – *les pays surendettés* = debt-burdened, *surprotéger* = to over-protect, *une star surmédiatisée* = with excessive media coverage.
   ultra – examples – *ultraconfus* = hopelessly confused, *ultrasimplifiée* = extremely simplified, *ultraperfectionné* = ultra-sophisticated.
   Less common prefixes to be included here are **macro, maxi**.

Examples
   Prefixes denoting a small degree –
   micro, mini, sous
   micro – examples – *un micro-émetteur* = micro-transmitter, *un micro-Etat* = mico-state, *un micro-problème* = minor problem.
   mini – examples – *une minicrise* = minor crisis, *une mini-croisière* = mini-cruise, *un miniscandale* = miniscandal.
   sous – examples – *sous-représenté* = under-represented, *une sous-évaluation* = under-estimation, *sous-peuplé* = under-populated.

Examples
   Prefixes denoting a number or a multiplicity –
   bi, demi, mono, tri, multi, pluri, poly.
   bi – examples – *un bicorps* = two-volume, *bi-emploi* = dual purpose, *la bipolarisation* = (bi)polarisation.
   demi – examples – *une demi-finale* = semi-final, *un demi-tarif* = half-fare, *une demi-volée* = half-volley.
   mono – examples – *monocanon* = single barrel, *une monoexportation* = single product exporting, *un monoréacteur* = single-engined jet aircraft.

tri – examples – *un tricorps* = three-volume, *un triréacteur* = three-engined jet.

multi – examples – *multicompétent* = multi-skilled, *le multipartisme* = multi-party system, *la multirisque* = all risks / comprehensive insurance.

pluri – examples – *pluriculturel* = multicultural, *pluriethnique* = multiethnic, *le pluripartisme* = multi-party system.

poly – examples – *polyhandicapé* = with multiple disabilities, *polylingue* = multilingual, *polyinsaturé* = polyunsaturate.

Prefixes relating to science or technology

- An amazing number of prefixes have been used in the 20th century to denote scientific advances or discoveries, many with a clear Greek or Latin origin.

In the following list, normally just one example will be given for each prefix.

Examples

aéro – *l'aérodynamisme* = aerodynamics.
agro – *l'agroalimentaire* = food-processing industry.
audio – *une audioconférence.*
bio – *biomédical.*
cryo – *la cryochirurgie* = cryosurgery (low-temperature).
chrono – *la chronobiologie* = study of bio-rhythms.
dermo – *la dermo-cosmétologie* = skin and beauty care.
électro – *l'électroménager* = household electrical appliances.
géo – *la géopolitique* = geopolitics.
hémo – *un hémo-test* = blood test.
hydro – *l'hydromassage* = hydromassage.
immuno – *un agent immunosuppresseur* = immunosuppressive.
magnéto – *la magnéto-optique* = magneto-optics.
neuro – *la neuroscience* = neuro-science.
paléo – *la paléopathologie* = paleopathology.
photo – *une photocopieuse* = photocopier.
psycho – *un psychopharmacologue* = psychopharmacologist.
techno – *un technoparc* = techno-park.
turbo – *le turboforage* = turbodrilling.

Polyvalent prefixes
- One or two prefixes have more than one value.
Examples

télé is ambiguous because it can (1) mean 'at a distance' and preserves its original meaning, (2) be a shortened form of *télévision* or (3) of *téléphone* (see below for further discussion of word shortening), and in both these cases the meaning of the deleted element is transferred to the prefix.

- *Examples*
    télétravail = teleworking, *téléchargement* = remote loading.
    une télépièce = play for television, *téléprêcheur* = telly evangelist.
    téléopérateur = telephone operator, *une télécarte* = phone card.
- *auto* can be (1) an abbreviation of *automobile*, but (2) much more often it retains its original meaning = self (as it does in the long form *automobile*).

Examples
    un autoradio = car radio, *une autoécole* = driving school.
    l'autodétestation = self-hate, *s'autoquereller* = to quarrel among themselves.
- *radio* is used as a truncated form of (1) *radiodiffusion* = broadcasting, or (2)of *radiographie* or (3) of *radioactif*.

Examples
    un *radio-taxi, radiotélévisé* = broadcast both on the radio and television.
    la radiodermite = radiodermititis, *un radiophysicien* = X-ray physicist.
    radio-élément, un radio-isotope.

— *Miscellaneous prefixes*

- There is still a large number of prefixes unaccounted for, some of which seem to be fairly loosely connected.
- *Some refer to time –*
    après – *l'après–2000* = post-millennium, *l'après-mousson* = post-monsoon.
    néo – *le néo-puritanisme*.
    péri – *péri-informatique* = computer environment.
    post – *le post-krach*.
    pré – *préprogrammer*.
- *Others to position* (allowing 'position' a wide meaning) –
    en – *enturbanner* = to put a turban on.
    extra – *extramuros* = out of town.
    inter – *interbancaire* = inter-bank, *interethnique*.
    outre – *outre-Méditerrané* = on the other side of the Mediterranean.
    para – *paracommercial*.
    sub – *subsaharien*.

— *Recent productive prefixes*
- Other prefixes have spawned many neologisms in recent years.
- *euro* is sometimes an abbreviation of (1) *Europe*, sometimes of (2) the *Union Européenne*.

Examples
    européaniser, eurovision.
    eurodéputés, europarlementaires; it has reached its apotheosis in being used to designate the new currency, *l'euro*.
    éco – *l'écosocialisme* = green socialism, *un écomusée* = museum devoted to the environment.

> *ethno* – *l'ethnomusicologie.*
> *narco* – *un narco-terroriste* = drug terrorist.
> *pétro* – *un pétro-dollar.*
- Old but still productive prefixes –
  > *re* can be attached to virtually any already existing word (see Chapter 3).
  > *co* – *un coanimateur* = co-presenter.
  > *pro* – *progouvernemental.*

Reprefixation

- Occasionally a neologism is produced by replacing a prefix on a well-established word by different one.

Examples

> *consensus* > *dissensus* = area of disagreement, *convolution* > *involution* = regression, *recrutement* > *décrutemen* = out-placement (helping workers to find another job).

Exercise

It was claimed earlier that derivation is a neat and economical way of creating new words. Using some of the examples of prefixation given above, how would you confirm – or deny – such a claim?

Suffixation

Suffixation

Whereas prefixation involved appending elements to the beginning of an already existing word, suffixation involves appending an element at the end of an already existing word.

Whereas it is convenient to classify prefixes by their meanings, it is more usual to classify suffixes by the word class they help produce.

Suffixation and verbs

- The situation regarding the formation of new verbs is very straightforward – only the first conjugation (verbs ending in *–er*) is productive.
- The only new examples belonging to the second conjugation which have been created in the 20th century are *alunir, amerrir,* which are clearly modelled on the much older *atterrir.*
- In these cases a prefix has been added to the original word at the same time as the suffix.
- The addition of *-er* has led to the creation of a very large number of new verbs. Some of the stems to which it is added are traditional French ones.

- Others come from a variety of other sources.

Examples

> *archiver* = to file, *patoiser* = to speak in a patois, *graffiter* = to paint graffiti, *scrabbler* = to play Scrabble.

- Sometimes the simple *-er* is supported by another element, producing a number of new verbs ending in *-ifier, -iser* in recent years.

Examples

> *complexifier* = to complicate, *fluidifier* – to fluidise, *charteriser* = to charter, *maximiser* = to maximise.

Suffixation and adverbs

- There is of course only one adverbial suffix in French, *-ment;* consequently there is little scope for originality. Even so, one or two fairly striking new adverbs have appeared – but how long, or if, they will survive is a different matter.

Examples

> *démentiellement* = insanely, *majoritairement* = for the most part, *prioritairement* = as a priority.

Suffixation and nouns and adjectives 1

- It is with nouns and adjectives that suffixation really comes into its own. A selection will have to be made, as the number of different suffixes involved is considerable.
- Suffixes denoting agents, activities and collections.
    Amongst the most common suffixes denoting agents are –
    -aire, -ard, -eur / -euse, -ien, -iste.
    less common are –
    -crate, -esse, -logue, -mane, -naute, -phile, -phobe.
- It will be noticed that *o* is often used as a linking element.
    Two examples will be provided for the more common suffixes, one for the others.
    -aire – *un décisionnaire* = decision-maker, *un gestionnaire* = administrator.
    -ard – (normally with a pejorative value) *un laïcard* = supporter of secularism, *un soixante-huitard* = veteran of the 1968 protests.

Suffixation and nouns and adjectives 2

> **-eur / -euse** – *un blablateur* = waffler, *un pacageur* = packager; *une rockeuse* = rock'n'roll fan, *une shooteuse* = junkie.
> **-ien** – *un pentathlonien* = pentathlete, *un plasticien* = plastic surgeon.
> **-iste** – *un documentaliste* = archivist, *un bédéiste* = cartoonist.
> **-crate** – *un hétérocrate* = someone dominated by heterosexual values.
> **-esse** – *une monstresse.*
> **-logue** – *un argotologue* = slang expert.
> **-mane** – *un wagnéromane* = Wagner fan.
> **-naute** – *un cybernaute* = cybernaut.
> **-phile** – *un jazzophile* = jazz lover

-phobe – *un bruxellophobe* = eurosceptic.
- Some fascinating new creations based on *-phile* occur –
  un copocléphile = collector of key rings, *un glicophile* = collector of sugar wrappers.

Exercise
  What is *un bédéphile, un matouphile, un télécartophile?*

Suffixation and nouns and adjectives 3
- **Suffixes denoting activities 1**
  -age, -ation, -ement, -isme, -ite, -ité, -itude, -lâtrie, -logie, -manie, -phobie.
  -age – *le formattage* = formatting, *le parrainage* = sponsorship.
  -ation – *la loubardisation* = descent into thuggery, *la starisation* = elevation to star status.
  -ement – *le défraiement* = payment of expenses, *le voilement* = wearing the (Islamic) veil.
  -isme – *le catastrophisme* = catastrophism, *l'hexagonalisme* = excessive French nationalism.
  -ite – *la bétonnite* = frenzied building activity, *la tégévite* = high speed train mania.
- **Suffixes denoting activities 2**
  -ité – *la garcité* = bitchiness, *la réactivité* = excitability.
  -itude – *la francitude* = Frenchness, *la maigritude* = thinness.
  -lâtrie – *la mitterrandolâtrie* = hero worship of François Mitterrand.
  -logie – *la bébéologie* = study of babies, *la contactologie* = science of contact lenses.
  -manie – *la groupusculomanie* = mania for forming splinter groups, *la muséomanie* = museum madness.
  -phobie – *la nippophobie* = fear of Japan, *la téléphobie* = television phobia.
- **Suffixes denoting collections**
  -arium, -at, -erie, -thèque
  -arium – *un instrumentarium* = synthesiser, *un insectarium* = insect house.
  -at – *le fonctionnariat* = civil service, *le lectorat* = readership.
  -erie – *une bouquinisterie* = second-hand bookshop, *une déchetterie* = waste collection centre.
  -thèque – *une cellulothèque* = blood-cell bank, *une ludothèque* = games library.

Suffixation and adjectives 1(a large group)
- Some of them have a (quasi-)scientific flavour –
  -gène, -cole, -phone, -phage, -vore.
  -gène – *criminogène* = encouraging crime.
  -cole – *aquacole* = aquicultural.
  -phone – *néerlandophone* = Dutch-speaking.

-phage – *téléphage* = addicted to watching TV.
-vore – *télévore* = addicted to watching TV.

Suffixation and adjectives 2
- Other suffixes have a less easily classifiable meaning which may be defined as 'associated with, related to' –
  -able / -ible, -aire, -ais, -al, -atif, -atoire, -el, -esque, -eux, -ien, -if, -ique, -iste, -istique.
  -able / -ible – *diffusable* = able to be broadcast, *constructible* = suitable for building.
  -aire – *postmortuaire* = relating to a post mortem, *télévisionnaire* = television.
  -ais (used with proper names) – *burundais* = Burundian, *hongkongais* = Hong Kong.
  -al – *libidinal, mandarinal* = relating to the establishment (ironical).
  -ard (normally with a pejorative value) – *ramenard* = big mouth.
  -atif – *récapitulatif* = summarising.
  -atoire – *masturbatoire* = masturbatory.
  -el – *gravitationnel, informationnel.*
  -esque – *himalayesque* = gigantic, *jargonnesque* = jargon-ridden.
  -eur – *activateur* = activating, *introspecteur* = introspective.
  -eux – *crapoteux* = toadlike.
  -ien – *malien* = Malian, *tontonien* = due to 'Tonton' (= President Mitterrand, see below).
  -if – *réactif* = quick to react.
  -ique – *hédonique* = full of pleasure, *pharonique* = extravagant.
  -iste – *consensualiste* = favouring consensus politics, *parisianiste* = Parisian-style.
  -istique – *capitalistique* = dependent on capital.

Suffixation and adjectives 3
- Still other suffixes have a more specific value –
  -issime, -mane, -phobe.
  -issime = excessive (often ironical) – *importantissime, snobissime.*
  -mane = lover of – *lyricomane.*
  -phobe = hater of, shy of – *néophobe, publiphobe.*

Suffixes appearing as prefixes
- Very rarely an affix which is normally a suffix appears as a prefix.
Examples
  -phile – *un philopin* = pin's (= badge) collector, *le philosémitisme* = prosemitism, *philorévolutionnaire* = pro-revolutionary.

Resuffixation
- Another fairly rare phenomenon is **resuffixation:** this occurs when a word, already composed through suffixation, has the suffix deleted and replaced by another, usually with a low register value.

> *Examples*
> *alsacien > alsako, portugais > portosse, télé > téloche, variétés > variétoche* = light music.

Composition

Sometimes the dividing line between derivation and composition is somewhat blurred: what is considered a prefix or suffix by some is considered an independent lexeme by others.

Composition

In principle **composition** is the process whereby two independent words are joined together to form a new single lexeme.

The process takes a number of forms in French and in some ways is rather anarchic, with all sorts of bizarre creations which do not conform to any general pattern.

Composition 1
- Words may be fused together more or less exactly as they are, that is without significant adjustment of form (however, a final 'mute' may be lost in the process).

Examples
> *énergivorace* = energy-consuming, *malvie* = poor quality of life, *rhônalpin*, *une vidéotransmission*.
> *aquaboniste* = defeatist; here three words have been combined plus the addition of a suffix (= < *à quoi bon* + *iste*).

- Many formations are **nonce words** – i.e. they are formed for particular effect at a particular moment, but are unlikely ever to be used again

Example
> *tontonmaniaque* was coined to describe ardent admirers of President Mitterrand (referred to as *tonton* = uncle), but with a future that is clearly bleak.

- *Use with place names*
  In a series of cases a place name involving a multiple lexeme produces a single-word adjective incorporating the elements of the place name but in an unfamiliar order; it also sometimes happens that the place name is recomposed and slightly latinised.

Examples
> *Bourg-la-Reine > réginaborgien, Fontainebleau > bellifontain, Ile-de-France > francilien, Pont-à-Mousson > mussipontain, Pont-Saint-Esprit > spiripontain.*
> Partial latinisation also occurs in examples such as *l'horodatage* = recording of time.

Composition 2
- More common than the previous scenario is that where two, and sometimes more, words, previously independent, are joined by a hyphen to denote a new concept. The following sub-categories provide some idea of the scope of this particular type of compound.

Examples 1
(1) The two words have equal value in the compound –
un spectateur-auditeur = viewer, *une fusée sol-air* = ground-to-air missile, *ni-ni* = policy of no further nationalisation, *un prospecteur-placier* = job-finder, *vrai-faux* = something which appears not to be what it is.
(2) One word has adjectival value –
un bateau-usine = factory ship, *une cité-satellite* = satellite town, *un homme grenouille* = frogman, *l'aïoli-rock* = rock music from Marseille, *un congé-formation* = training leave, *un roman-BD* = strip-cartoon novel, *le gouvernement nord-coréen* = North Korean, *les pays latins-américains* = Latin-American.
(3) A phrase may also be hyphenated turning it into a more cohesive expression. Various possibilities exist –
the first element is a preposition –
    les hors-travail = unemployed, *les sans-papiers* = illegal immigrant workers, *à-plat* = flat tint, *un entre-deux-vols* = stop-over, *un à-valoir* = down payment, *un contre-la-montre* = race against the clock.
the second element is an adverb –
    le parler-faux = double talk, *le parler-vrai* = straight talking.

Examples 2
- Very common is a combination where the first element is a verb –
un chauffe-eau = water-heater, *un sèche-cheveux* = hair-drier, *un pare-douche* = shower cubicle, *un pare-sida* = AIDS-preventer, *porte-instruments* = instrument-carrying, *un repose-jambes* = foot-rest.
- Other types of combinations –
un pas-de-chance = no-hoper, *un père-la-rigueur* = stickler for discipline, *un père-la-morale* = holier than thou, *le va-t-à-la-messe* = church going, *va-t'en-guerre* = gung-ho, *l'être-ensemble* = togetherness.
- On the analogy of *prêt-à-porter* = ready-to-wear come by analogy a whole series of similar hyphenated phrases –
prêt-à-voir = off-the-peg (spectacles), *prêt-à-jeter* = disposable (goods), *prêt-à-écouter* = easy listening (music).

Exercise
Using the verb + noun pattern, find the French for *dish-washer, drill, windscreen, car bumper*.

Composition 3

- This group of compounds involves two, and sometimes more, words being linked by an *-o*.
- In the written form, if just two words are involved, the words often occur as a single unit (i.e. without a hyphen), underlining the integrated nature of the compound.
- When more than three words are combined in this way, there is the danger of mental overload, as the hearer / reader attempts to hold an excessive number of concepts in his / her mind at the same time.
- These compounds generally evoke a pedantic tone.

Examples

> *l'afropessimisme* = pessimism about Africa, *un narcotrafiquant* = drugs dealer, *pharmacodépendant (? prefix)* = drugs dependent, *pifométrique* = intuitive, *vitrocéramique* = ceramic, *occidentalocentrisme* = preocupation with the West, *un primo-arrivant* = new arrival, *un primo-migrant* = first generation immigrant, *ibéro-américain* = Latin-American, *câblo-opérateur* = cable (TV) company, *hospitalo-universitaire* = university hospital, *islamo-progressiste* = Islamic progressive, *la manico-dépression* = chronic depression, *les relations israélo-arabes* = Arab-Israeli.
>
> *des explications poético-psychologico-métaphysico-mystiques.*

Composition – linking elements

- It occasionally happens that *i* is used instead of *o* as the link.

Examples

> *céréaliculture* = cereal production, *gréviculture* = habit of striking, *riziculture* = *rice production.*

Composition 4

- Other combinations occur which are not linked by a hyphen and / or are not linked by an *i / o* and which, therefore, are looser in formation.
- Because the combinations seem to function as single mental entities, despite the fact that in formal orthography they are not integrated, they will be treated under the compound heading.
- A number of possibilities exist.

Examples

> noun + preposition + noun, of which there are many, many examples –
>> *le garde au sol* = road holding, *la mise sous cloche* = putting on the back-burner, *la gestion de patrimoine* = personal portfolio management, *un produit d'appel* = loss leader, *un député de base* = backbencher, *un placement d'attente* = short-term investment, *une imprimante à jet d'encre* = bubble-jet printer, *une carte à mémoire, un mouchoir en papier* = paper handkerchief, *une planche à voile* = wind-surfer.
>
> noun + adjective, again very common –
>> *une famille élargie* = extended family, *un pot catalytique* = catalytic

> converter, *une axe rouge* = clearway, *un pirate informatique* = computer
> hacker, *la remontée capillaire* = rising damp, *le non-remplacement des
> départs* = natural wastage, *un cheveu lingual* = hair-lip.

noun + noun; this combination is very close (if not identical with ellipsis,
discussed below) –

> *une date butoir* = deadline, *la gauche caviar* = champagne socialist, *le génie
> logiciel* = software engineering.

verb + noun –

> *un tue l'amour* = turn-off.

Word shortenings

Not only are new words formed by adding already existing elements together,
other new words come into being through the deletion of an element. This proce-
dure is known as word shortening. A number of processes are involved, which go
from the loss of a single sound, to the loss of a syllable to the loss of all but the initial
letters of word groups, complex lexemes. They all illustrate one of the major trends
of modern French, which is the desire to communicate as economically and effi-
ciently as possible, discarding certain sounds which are not essential to compre-
hension. The most convenient way to examine them is under the following
headings:

Sigles, Acronyms, Truncation, Ellipsis, Blends

Sigle

> This process involves abbreviation by initial letters.

Sigles – history
- The process was rare before the 19th century, and sigles did not appear in
  domains where they seem to be absolutely essential nowadays, especially in
  newspapers, with reference to political parties, trades unions and other
  organisations, until the Second World War.
- Sporting vocabulary seems to have been the major instigator of early examples, from where the process moved into the military and commercial
  domains.
- In these early examples, the abbreviated form did not appear until well after
  the full form had been in existence for some time.
- Nowadays, the two forms, the full and the abbreviated, appear simultaneously. What is extremely common, in the press, is for the abbreviated form
  to take precedence over the full form, and for the latter to be provided in
  parentheses after the abbreviated form.
- In fact sigles are essentially the product of the written medium rather than of
  speech.

Examples (*a small selection*)

- Examples abound in the realms of *trade unions* –
  CGT = Confédération générale du travail, FO = Force ouvrière.
- *Education* –
  CEG = collège d'enseignement général, CES = collège d'enseignement secondaire,
  CET = collège d'enseignement technique.
- *Commercial enterprises and practices* –
  BNP = Banque nationale de Paris, CL = Crédit lyonnais, PDG = président-
  directeur général, PME = petites et moyennes entreprises, VPC = vente par
  correspondance.
- *National institutions and services* –
  SNCF = Société des chemins de fer français, PTT = Postes, télécommunications et
  télédiffusion, RMI = revenu minimum d'insertion, TGV = train à grande vitesse.
- *Political parties* –
  PC = Parti communiste, PS = Parti socialiste, RPR = Rassemblement pour la
  République, UDF = Union pour la démocratie française.
- Less technically, *les SDF = sans domicile fixe* and *les VTT = vélos tout terrain* are
  all part of the landscape.
- Whereas a few years ago the names of a number of *countries* were denoted by
  initial letters (for example, *RDA = République démocratique allemande, RFA =*
  République fédérale allemande), the United States is now the only country regu-
  larly denoted in such a way – *E-U = Etats-Unis* (even *USA*).

Exercise

Discover the full forms of the following sigles and assign them to one of the
above groupings – or, if necessary, suggest extra groupings –

EU, IVG, ONG, RATP, RER, TF1, BCBG, HS, TVA.

Sigles and pronunciation

- It should also be noted that there are certain sigles which appear only in the
  written form and are never pronounced. These sometimes consist of more
  than just the initial letter(s) – *bvd, exp = expéditeur, F = féminin, kg, M., Mme, svp.*

Acronym

Acronyms are a subgroup of sigles, the difference being that the letters constituting the former may be pronounced as single words, whereas the letters
constituting the latter are pronounced individually.

This means that acronyms may sometimes be treated as conventional words;
this possibility is emphasised when the combination appears in lower case
script.

Acronyms – history

- Acronyms did not come onto the scene until after the Second World War, but have become more and more common in recent years. Occasionally one has the impression that the abbreviated form was conceived first and a long form invented to fit it!

Examples

Amongst the best known examples are –

capès = certificat d'aptitude au professorat de l'enseignement du second degré, ovni = objet volant non-identifié = UFO, *sida = syndrome immuno-déficitaire acquis* = AIDS, *smic = salaire minimum interprofessionnel de croissance.*

Some are borrowed from English, e.g. *laser, radar.*

Names of national and international organisations proliferate and are often denoted by acronyms –

FNAC = Fédération des achats des cadres, OTAN = Organisation du traité de l'Atlantique du nord, ONU = Organisation des Nations unies, OPEP = Organisation des pays exportateurs de pétrole, INSERM = Institut national de la santé et de la recherche médicale, INSEE = Institut national de la statistique et des études économiques, ORSEC = Organisation des secours, SOFRES = Société française des enquêtes par sondage.

Some organisations retain an English acronym in French, e.g. *UNESCO, YMCA.* More recent examples are –

le PAF = paysage audiovisuel français; le tuc = travail d'utilité collective, NAP = Neuilly-Auteuil-Passy, the equivalent of the British *yuppy.*

Sigles and antonyms and derivatives

- With both sigles and more especially acronyms, it is possible to form derivatives, as if the abbreviated form was a base in its own right.

Examples

words derived from sigles –

cégétiste, vététiste, RMIstes.

words derived from acronyms –

onusien, sidéen = suffering from AIDS, *sidénologue* = AIDS specialist, *tuciste.*

Blends

Blend

A **blend** is the result of **truncation and composition** – elements of two words are lost and what remains is joined to form a new word.

Many of such creations have a technical ring about them, since they are formed to describe a scientific discovery which unites two processes or two items.

Examples

Probably the best known example of a blend is *franglais* < *français* + *anglais*.

Other examples

progiciel < *programme* + *logiciel*, *plapier* < *papier* + *plastique*, *fanzine* < *fanatique* + *magazine*, *foultitude* < *foule* + *multitude*.

- It seems that often this type of blend is invented by journalists as a source of humour and consequently has only a short life-expectancy.

Exercises

What do you think are the original two forms which make up *frantalien*, *francitan*?

What forms were involved in creating the following blends? –

célibattante = militant unmarried feminist, *plasturgie* = plastic surgery, *tapuscrit* = typed script, *zapanthrope* = disillusioned (TV) channel switcher.

Ellipsis

Ellipsis

Words which carry little semantic information are deleted from an expression – often grammatical tool words – the context generally being sufficiently clear to prevent confusion. Even without a context, the words juxtaposed regularly succeed in informing on each other, and the connection between them is soon discerned.

This process is also much loved by journalists, as like blends and sigles, it speeds up the delivery of a message.

Examples 1

la pause déjeuner = lunch break, *le trafic poids lourd* = heavy goods traffic, *fin septembre* = the end of September, *un prix choc* = rock-bottom price, *une touche effacement* = delete key, *une ville fantôme* = ghost town.

Examples 2

- Sometimes a seemingly more vital part of an expression is lost –
- For example the first noun in a complex lexeme may disappear, leaving the qualifying element (adjective or noun group) to take over the role played by the head word –

la ville capitale > *la capitale*, *un bateau à vapeur* > *un vapeur*, *un costume à deux-pièces* > *un deux-pièces*, *un fromage de Brie / de Camembert, etc.* > *un brie, camembert, etc.*, *les élections législatives / présidentielles / européennes, etc.* > *les législatives / présidentielles / européennes, etc.* and more recently, *les chaussures de basket* > *les baskets* = trainers.

Ellipsis and false anglicisms
- Ellipsis is in fact the source of many so-called false anglicisms in French: one element of an English lexeme, often the main sense-bearing component, is dropped and its sense transferred to the remaining element.

Examples

  la holding (company), le compact (disc), le skin (head), le sweat (shirt).

Truncation

Truncation

Truncation, or clipping, as it is also know, involves the suppression of certain sounds, usually, but not always, a whole syllable or syllables, from a word and retaining the rest of the word. The syllables or sounds retained are normally those which on the one hand bear the most information and which on the other have a relatively low frequency: in other words, the element retained is retained because it is less likely to fall victim to homonymy.

Truncation – history
- Some truncations go back a long way and are so well established that they have replaced their full counterparts, and speakers are barely aware that a longer form exists. Indeed using the longer forms would sound pedantic and pompous.
- Truncations are very much part of casual speech, found especially in the mouths of young people.

Exercise

What are the original forms of the following well-established truncations? –

métro, cinéma, photo, pneu, vélo.

There are a number of points of interest to note.

Position of the break
- There seems to be no restriction on the position of the break, sometimes at a morpheme boundary, usually after a prefix, but it may equally well occur later on in the word, and may even cut across morpheme boundaries.

Exercise

Sort the following examples into the appropriate categories – break at morpheme boundary, break later on in word, break within morpheme –

séropo, info, micro, amphi, survêt, préado, pub.

Final sounds
- As far as the final sound of a truncation is concerned, it is usually a vowel and usually *-o*.

Truncation and suffixation
- Truncation is sometimes combined with suffixation. This seems to happen primarily when there is not already an *-o* in the word for which a truncation is sought. Consequently the word is cut at a convenient point and a new suffix, in *-o*, added.

Examples
> *intellectuel* does not include an *-o*, but such is the popularity of that sound in word-final position that one is added – *intellectuel > intello*.
> Similarly, *socialiste > socialo, technicien > technico*.

- Ironically in the last two cases the original number of syllables is restored (so much for the urge to save effort!).

Exercise
Compound lexemes are not immune to this process, sometimes resulting in unusual forms. What do you think the original forms of the following truncations of compound lexemes are? –

> *aprèm, beauf, prêtap, petit-déj.*

(Hint – think of a time of day, a relation, off-the-peg clothes and a meal.)

Word-shortening and ambiguity
- A problem that is common to certain of these types of word-shortening is ambiguity. The shorter a word, the more likely it is have a homonym.

Examples
> *ME = machine à écrire, musée d'ethnographie.*
> *micro = microphone, micro-ordinateur, four à micro-ondes.*
> *PAF = paysage audiovisuel français, police de l'air et des frontières.*

Exercise
In some of these cases, gender saves the day – how?

Verlan

Verlan is the newest of the processes to be reviewed in this chapter.

Verlan

Verlan involves the inversion of the syllables or sounds in a word (occasionally a phrase). *Verlan* itself is the result of the inversion of the syllables of *l'envers* = back-to-front.

Verlan – history
- Although sporadic examples exist from the late 19th century, it was not until the end of the 1970s that it became common, first in Paris and then spreading to other urban areas.
- Verlan is associated mainly with disaffected young people, who try to disguise the meaning of their words by making them impenetrable to adults and other uninitiated outsiders.

Verlanisation 1
- In phrases consisting of two words, the words are reversed –

Examples
> *comme ça > ça comme, par terre > terre par, fais voir > vwarf* (with deletion of the final syllable).

- In words of two syllables, the two syllables are interchanged –

Examples
- Since verlan is essentially an oral phenomenon, the orthography of the neologisms is not always certain.
> *barjot = jobard* = gullible, *béton = tomber (laisse béton!* = forget it!*), chébran = branché* = with it, *ripou = pourri* = corrupt, *tromé = métro, zarbi = bizarre.*

- Words of three syllables are less often involved –

Example
> *garetsi = cigarette.*

- In monosyllabic words, the form of the new word depends upon whether (1) an open syllable (i.e. the word ends in a vowel) or (2) a closed syllable (i.e. the word ends in a consonant) is involved.
- In (1) the sounds are inverted –

Examples
> *chaud > och, fou > ouf, pied > yep, pue > up* = stink.

Verlanisation 2
- In (2), there are three possibilities –
> (a) if the word ends in a mute *e*, the *e* is sounded, and the resulting two syllables, are reversed and the second syllable is deleted.

Examples
> *femme* > **femmeu* > **meufem* > *meuf* (* = hypothetical, unattested form), *mère*
> > *rem, père* > *rep*.

- (b) a new syllable in / ə / is added to words which do not end in mute *e*, and the syllables are reversed.

Examples
> *dur* > *redu, taf* > *feuta* = fag, *tronche* > *chetron*.

- (c) the same process occurs as in (b), except that the final syllable is deleted.
- *Examples*
  > *flic* > *keuf, mec* > *keum*.

The rules of verlanisation

- The above has been a simplification of the rules. In fact, the rules themselves are not without exceptions, the most notable being –
  arabe > *beur*.
  where the first syllable of the original term is also deleted.

Reverlanisation

- Verlanisation is a living process which continues to evolve.
- Words that have been verlanised once become reverlanised – in other words, if a word becomes familiar to those who are not supposed to understand it, it is modified by the *verlanisants* in order to keep the code cryptic.

Examples
> *flic* > *keuf* > *feukeu, arabe* > *beur* > *rebeu*.

Change of Meaning

Many of the same considerations apply here as when changes of meaning were discussed in relation to developments in Vulgar Latin (in Chapter 3), namely that it is extremely difficult to classify them satisfactorily. Categories are broad and based upon the mechanics of the process rather than upon the meaning processes themselves.

Certain trends are discernible in French neologisms. However, it should be stressed firstly that it is not always possible to place certain neologisms squarely in a particular category, secondly that certain neologisms seem to belong to more than one category and thirdly that the categories are not so distinct as might be desired (e.g. generalisation of meaning at times comes very close to metaphorical usage; specialisation of meaning often involves transference of a word from use in one specialised sphere to another).

Generalisation of meaning

Examples
> *abouti* = successful (originally only past participle of *aboutir* = to succeed).
> *boulimique* = compulsive, e.g. *un collectionneur boulimique* (*la boulimie* = compulsive eating).
> *cartonner* = to be a hit (originally = to bind (i.e. embellish) a book).

décapant = revealing (e.g. *une photographie décapante*) (originally *décaper* = to scour).

un intégriste = whole-hearted supporter (originally = fundamentalist with religious connotation).

surfer = to coast, to freewheel.

tétaniser = to paralyse, to reduce to inaction, also to stimulate (originally only = to tetanise).

tonique = breezy (e.g. *une femme tonique*) (originally relating to health).

un turbo = driving force (e.g. *les rapatriés ont été le turbo de la France des années 70*).

le zapping = moving from one form of entertainment to another (originally restricted to changing television stations).

Specialisation of meaning

Examples

l'assistance = (emergency) assistance (for break-downs, etc.).

une brève = news bite (or perhaps ellipsis).

une chaîne = television channel.

les armes conventionnelles = non-nuclear weapons.

gauchir = to move to the left (politically).

numérique = digital (originally = numerical).

une piste = runway, ski slope.

une raffinerie = oil refinery.

spécialisé = dedicated (of computers).

tourner = to make a film.

Metaphor

Examples

les barrages = play-offs (in sport) (originally = barrier to progress).

être en béton = to be safe (= made of concrete).

avoir une langue de bois = to use clichéd expressions.

une cascade = film stunt.

une comète = a rising star (extending idea of *star*).

un travail de chartreux = painstaking work (*les Chartreux* = monks).

les dents de scie = ups and downs (of life).

geler = to take out of production.

un tremblé = a wavy line.

son vaisseau d'amiral = his flagship (e.g. of hotel, product).

It is interesting to note how certain domains are particularly productive of metaphors.

Centres of metaphoric attraction

- Many names of *animals* have been enlisted to denote human types (in addition to those which have been in existence for a long time and those which have a universal application, e.g. *les colombes et les faucons* = doves and hawks).

Examples

> *un crocodile* = shark, *un éléphant* = die hard, *un gorille* = bodyguard; associated with these are words like *un kangarou* = baby sling, *un cocon* = safe seat (in the *Assemblée Nationale).*

- In addition, there are metaphorical expressions with *culinary associations* –

Examples

> *la cerise sur le gâteau* = the cherry on the cake, *mettre les bouchées doubles* = to work twice as hard.

- with **military associations**

> *être dans le colimateur* = to have your sights on someone, *monter au créneau* = to step into the breach, *rectifier le feu* = to adjust your aim

- with *domestic associations*

Examples

> *jeter le bébé avec l'eau du bain* = to throw the baby out with the bathwater, *enfoncer le clou* = to ram the point home, *renverser la vapeur* = to turn the tables, *avoir plusieurs casquettes* = to wear several hats (= to have several responsibilities).

Metonymy

Examples

> *la blanche* = nickname for *gendarmerie départementale* (based upon the colour of their épaulettes), heroine or cocaine.
>
> *bof* = apathetic (originally an interjection equivalent to a shrug of the shoulders, now used as an adjective).
>
> *le charbon* = hard work (used in extracting coal).
>
> *la galère* = difficult time (reminiscent of slaves rowing on a galley).
>
> *la piscine* = nickname for HQ of French Secret Services (opposite the *Piscine des Tourelles* in Paris).
>
> *une plume* = writer.
>
> *tremper son biscuit* = to dip his wick (sexual).
>
> *les Verts* = Green political party (through association with environmental concern).

Abstract nouns used to denote concrete items

Examples

> *la direction* = management.
>
> *la rédaction* = editorial board.
>
> *la vitesse* = gear (of car, etc.).

Hyperbole

Examples

> *une caricature* = mug (face).
>
> *éclater* = to disperse (e.g. *éclater un système devenu ingouvernable).*
>
> *s'enflammer* = to speak with passion.

géant = great.

planétaire = world-wide.

Change of word class

Examples

agir – verb > noun = action.

> e.g. la 'Théorie de l'agir communicationnel' est son oeuvre maîtresse. *Express*, 12.6.87

charrette – noun > adjective = overburdened.

> e.g. Charrette. Débordé. Exemple: 'Je suis charrette'. *Expansion*, 6.9.94.

classe – noun > adjective = stylish.

> e.g. ils étaient 'cheap', les 'synthés': ils deviennent classe. *Express*, 27.11.87.

fraîche – adjective > noun = cool of the morning.

> e.g. Autrefois réservés à l'heure de l'apéritif, ils [TV games shows] assaillent les lucarnes à la fraiche. Dès 10 heures du matin. *Express*, 22.11.85.

Conclusion

And so, with the inventiveness of modern French ringing in our ears, we have reached the end of the challenge of grappling with French words. We have seen how they are constructed, we have seen how to define a word, we have seen where French words come from and the techniques being used to create new words. The message is that French has a noble history, drawing on the resources of many other languages to renew itself, as well as having an impressive array of internal devices at its disposal enabling it to create new words. The language is alive and well. It has the ability to keep abreast of current scientific and technical advances, of developments taking place throughout the world. For its birth it was reliant upon the forces at work in Gaul. Now, having reached maturity, it can bend the resources of other languages to suit its purposes and manipulate its own resources to continue to progress. May it be a source of inspiration to you.

Appendix

Answers to Exercises in Chapter 1

Exercise 1. *admettre, commettre, émettre, omettre, permettre, promettre, remettre, soumettre, transmettre.*

Exercise 2. *fortiche, fortifiant, fortification, fortifié, fortissimo.*Note that sometimes more than one morpheme is involved (*fort + -ifi- + -ant > fortifiant, fort + -ifi- + -cation > fortification*).

Exercise 3. *froidement, froideur, froidure, refroidir, refroidissement, refroidisseur; allongement, allonger, longer, longévité, longitude, longuement, longueur, rallonge, rallonger.*

Exercise 4. *capital + isme, dés + human+iser, en + soleill + é, re + tomb + é + e, rigour + euse + ment, sur + abond + ance.*

Exercise 5. You should be able to identify the following morphemes – *-e*: *fatal, grand, humain, lent, meilleur, petit; -euse: consciencieux, heureux, peureux; -trice: conservateur;* stem variation: *ancien, blanc, bon, complet, dernier, gentil, las, léger, muet, premier, secret, solennel, sot.*

Exercise 6. You should be able to identify the following morphemes – *-e*: *agent, avocat, étudiant, protestant; -esse: hôte, prince, ère: boulanger, fermier; -ine: héros; -euse: acheteur, danseur, vendeur; -trice: éditeur, exécuteur, moniteur;* stem variation: *chat, chien, époux, lion, veuf.*

Exercise 7. *-s: exercice, semaine, violent; -aux: animal, corail, normal, verbal; -x: bijou, cheveu, chou, pou, voeu.*

Exercise 8. *-ons, -ez, -ont.*

Exercise 12. *au* = two morphemes, *à la* = three morphemes, *aux* = two morphemes.

Answers to Exercises in Chapter 3

p.36. *bellus > beau / bel, rapidus > rapide, nudus > nu.*

p.37. *cantare > chanter, portare > porter, plorare > pleurer.*

p.38. *canem > chien, dormire > dormir, hibernum > hiver, mica > mie, patrem > père, lactem > lait, florem > fleur.*

p.42.

Vowel	Tonic		Countertonic	
	Blocked	*Free*	*Blocked*	*Free*
VL [i]		amicum, filum, servire		
VL [e]		credere, bibit, habere, me		pelare
VL [ɛ]		ferrum, novellum, porcellum	errare, servire	
VL [a]		clarum, errare, lavare, matrem, mortalem, pelare, probare		amicum, habere, lavare
VL [ɔ]		novem, soror	mortalem, porcellum	novellum, probare
VL [o]				
VL [u]		furorem		furorem

p.43. *annum > an, bon(i)tatem > bonté, cantat > chante, famem > faim, fontana > fontaine, frenum > frein, granum > grain, lentum > lent, linum > lin, pontem > pont, tentare > tenter, tonum > ton, venit > vient.*

p.44. *aquila > aigle, boscum > bois, canalem > chenal, capillos > cheveux, ecclesia > église, facere > faire, jacere > gésir, medianum > moyen, nocere > nuire, octo > huit, otiosum > oiseux, pejor > pire, rationem > raison, regalem > royal, sex > six, tectura > toit, tractare > traiter, troja > truie.*

p.46. consonants in strong position – *ardentem, caballum, carbonum, corona, donum, gustum, longum, privare, rupta, vita.* consonants in weak position – *ardentem, caballum, carbonum, corona, donum, gustum, longum, privare, rupta, vita.*

p.46. *scola > école, scribere > écrire, scutum > écu, spatha > épée, sponsum > époux, strictum > étroit.*

p.47. *carbonem > charbon, fleb(i)lem > faible, inflare > enfler, patrem > père, rupta > route, scriptum > écrit, servire > servir, sufflare > souffler, viv(e)re > vivre.*

p.47. *castellum > château, costa > côte, ess(e)re > être, gustum > goût, piscare > pêcher, spasmare > pâmer, testa > tête, vespa > guêpe.*

p.47. *caballum > cheval, carum > cher, cantare > chanter, centum > cent, cinerem > cendre, cubitum > coude, collum > col, cor > coeur, bucca > bouche, vacca > vache, peccatum > péché, porcellum > pourceau, rad(i)cina > racine.*

p.47. *cima > cime, corona > couronne, dolorem > douleur, farina > farine, finire > finir, fumat > fume, luna > lune, nova > neuve, parare > parer, tela > toile, lavare > laver.*

p.48. *avicellum > oiseau, augustum > août, caballum > cheval, debere > devoir, jocare > jouer, locare > louer, necare > noyer, nepotem > neveu, pacare > payer, placere > plaisir, probare > prouver, regina > reine, ripa > rive, rota > roue, ruga > rue, sudare > suer, videre > voir, viginti > vingt, vita > vie.*

p.49. *brevem > bref, caelum > ciel, capum > chef, carum > cher, cor > coeur, crudum > cru, florem > fleur, gratum > gré, hospitalem > hôtel, novum > neuf, ovum > oeuf, per > par, sal > sel, scutum > écu, solum > seul, vadum > gué.*

p.49. *diurnum > jour, jam > ja(mais), tibia > tige, sapiam > sache; agnellum > agneau, montanea > montagne, signa > signe, unionem > oignon, vinea > vigne.*

p.49. *habere > avoir, herba > herbe, hominem > homme, homo > on, hora > heure.*

p.59. *considérer* generalisation, = to contemplate the stars; *crétin* euphemism, = Christian; *cuisse* = thigh, metonymy through juxtaposition in space, < *coxa* = hip; *finance* specialisation, < *finir* = to bring to a conclusion; *pondre* specialisation, < *ponere* = to put down; *révéler* generalisation, = to remove a veil.

Bibliography

Battye, A. and Hintze, M.-A. (2000) *The French Language Today* (2nd edn). London: Routledge.

Brunet, E. (1981) *Le Vocabulaire français de 1789 à nos jours* (3 vols). Paris: Slatkine-Champion.

Brunot, F. (1905–1953) *Histoire de la langue française des origines à nos jours* (13 vols). Paris: Colin.

Calvet, L.-J. (1994) *L'Argot*. Paris: PUF Que Sais-Je?

Désirat, C. and Hordé, T. (1988) *La Langue française au 20e siècle*. Paris: Bordas.

Guilbert, L. (1975) *La Créativité lexicale*. Paris: Larousse.

Guiraud, P. (1965) *Les Mots étrangers*. Paris: PUF Que Sais-Je?

Guiraud, P. (1967) *Structures étymologiques du lexique français*. Paris: Larousse.

Hope, T.E. (1971) *Lexical Borrowing in the Romance Languages*. Oxford: Blackwell.

Mitterand, H. (1968) *Les Mots français*. Paris: PUF Que Sais-Je?

Nyrop, K. (1930–1968) *Grammaire historique de la langue française* (6 vols). Copenhagen: Glydendal.

Sanders, C. (1993) *French Today*. Cambridge: Cambridge University Press.

Walter, H. (1988) *Le Français dans tous les sens*. Paris: Robert Laffont.

Wise, H. (1997) *The Vocabulary of Modern French: Origins, Structure and Function*. London and New York: Routledge.

and many, many dictionaries!